KNOWING the
OLD TESTAMENT

KNOWING the
OLD TESTAMENT

BY JAMES P. BERKELEY

VALLEY FORGE

JUDSON PRESS ®

Foreword

THE WRITING of this brief Foreword to *Knowing the Old Testament* is a happy privilege. I have known Dr. James P. Berkeley, its author, somewhat intimately for many years, and my life has been much enriched by his Christian character, his helpful instruction, and his friendly counsel. Furthermore, I have come to have a great appreciation of his pioneer work in Christian education, his skill as a writer of curriculum material, and his wide and deeply spiritual biblical scholarship.

This book is not to be confused with any of the numerous books already in print which have as their expressed aim the acquainting of the reader with the Old Testament writings. Although these chapters do not neglect the familiar questions respecting authorship, date, and canonicity of the Old Testament books, they go far beyond such matters. Dr. Berkeley's primary concern is that the reader shall come to know vitally the God who is revealed in the Old Testament; that is to say, the eternal, holy, and merciful One who is the "God and Father of our Lord Jesus Christ." He makes it clear that the Old Testament, far from being an archaic and now largely obsolete book, is an essential part of God's revelation of himself to mankind. It is, indeed, the indispensable introduction to the New Testament. Neither Testament can be fully understood without a knowledge of the other.

Only a teacher of wide experience could express the profound theological concepts dealt with in this book in the simple, direct, and easy-to-read fashion found here. Although they are not discussed in detail, full account has been taken of the latest archaeological discoveries and textual researches. Also of much practical importance is the fact that the author has so organized his material that other teachers will find it easy to employ this book as a text. It abounds with wise pedagogical suggestions.

MILES W. SMITH

CONTENTS

1

2

3

4

5

6

7

8

1

JESUS USED THE OLD TESTAMENT

THE STARTING POINT for the Christian teacher of the Old
Testament is this important fact: *Jesus used the Old Testament.* As a child growing in wisdom (Luke 2:52) he was
taught the scriptures; that is to say, the Old Testament.
When he taught the people he used those writings. Because
Jesus found the Old Testament essential in his thinking,
living, and teaching, the Christian teacher also should learn
to use the Old Testament books in growing in wisdom.
Also he should become better trained in the use of them
in instructing others. Some Christians undervalue the Old
Testament, but Jesus said: "Think not that I have come to
abolish the law and the prophets; I have not come to abolish
them but to fulfill them" (Matt. 5:17). A Christian teacher
is Christ-centered in all things. Therefore the Christian
teacher uses the scriptures which Christ used. He will not
avoid the Old Testament because it seems too difficult or
too ancient. He will remember these words which Jesus
read in Psalm 119:105: "Thy word is a lamp to my feet
and a light to my path." This word that Jesus used was
the Old Testament.

1. WHAT WAS THE OLD TESTAMENT
WHICH JESUS USED?

In Luke 4:16-21 we find an illuminating picture of
Jesus using the Old Testament.

"And he came to Nazareth, where he had been brought up; and he went to the synagogue, as his custom was, on the sabbath day. And he stood up to read; and there was given to him the book of the prophet Isaiah. He opened the book and found the place where it was written,

'The Spirit of the Lord is upon me,
because he has anointed me to preach good news
   to the poor.
He has sent me to proclaim release to the captives
and recovering of sight to the blind,
to set at liberty those who are oppressed,
to proclaim the acceptable year of the Lord.'

And he closed the book, and gave it back to the attendant, and sat down; and the eyes of all in the synagogue were fiixed on him. And he began to say to them, "Today this scripture has been fulfilled in your hearing.'"

Observing carefully this incident, one can in imagination see Jesus and the scriptures. We see Jesus standing up in the synagogue, a teacher before his class. He asked for the scroll of Isaiah. There was a man in charge of the property of the synagogue. This man went to a box or chest, called the "ark," which contained the scrolls of holy writings owned by that synagogue. Selecting the scroll asked for, he brought it to Jesus. Jesus unrolled the scroll until he found the place from which he desired to read. After reading the passage, Jesus rolled up the scroll and returned it to the attendant who replaced it in the ark where it was carefully treasured. Here is the picture to get first in mind. It should be dramatized in imagination or may be acted out before a class.

In those days people did not have what we call "books," that is, volumes made up of pages written on both sides and bound together. A "book" for them was a scroll, a long sheet wound around itself on a spindle. Writing was upon parchment; i.e., the skins of animals, finished on one side for writing. Sheets were sewed together end to end to form one long, continuous document which was rolled up into a scroll. To read such a "book" required unrolling until the desired passage was found and then the rolling up again after the reading.

These rolls were kept very carefully in a chest. The many books of the Jewish scriptures could not be contained in one roll. The chest in the synagogue held a collection of these manuscripts, many different rolls. So Jesus asked for the particular writing which he desired to use. The attendant selected that one and brought it to Jesus. After the reading, he deposited it again for safekeeping.

When, therefore, we think of the form of the Old Testament in the days of Jesus, we must picture such a collection of rolls in a chest. All of them were written by hand, a long and difficult task for a writer. Because they had to be written in that slow, laborious way, one copy at a time, on parchment sheets, books were few in number and expensive. They were limited in distribution and could not be a common possession among the people. In the Temple and in the synagogue, however, they could be found, read, and studied. See the story of the boy Jesus in the Temple (Luke 2:41-47). The people who came to the synagogue in Nazareth did not bring their Bibles with them, nor did they find copies where they sat. Jesus did not bring a scroll with him. He and all the others came to hear and read the scrolls owned by that particular synagogue, copies which were carefully treasured under the care of the man appointed to that stewardship.

It was the custom of the Jewish people to gather in their meetings on their sabbaths to hear the reading of the Law and the Prophets. Note, "the utterances of the prophets which are read every sabbath" (Acts 13:27). Every Jew was carefully trained in the memorization of the scriptures both in the synagogue schools and in the sabbath services. Because they had no individual copies, they had to memorize the words. So they carried about in their memories a great deal of the writings, and, although they did not bring books to the meeting, they brought minds saturated with passages from the various rolls. It may be said that the Old Testament of Jesus' day existed largely in the well-trained memories of the people.

So when Jesus stood up and asked for the roll of Isaiah, accepted it from the hand of the attendant, unrolled it to the place he wanted, read from it, rerolled it, and returned it to the attendant, a solemn act full of the sense of the sacred was taking place in that house of prayer. The people followed his reading with sharp, well-stored memories. This roll of Isaiah was the most popular among the Prophets.

2. WHAT OTHER ROLLS WERE IN THE COLLECTION?

The Jews had a threefold collection: the Law, the Prophets, and the Writings. Learn the books in each of these collections.

The Law. This was regarded as one book, a fivefold book, the Pentateuch. To them it was a single unit, marked off into five divisions: Genesis, Exodus, Leviticus, Numbers, and Deuteronomy. It was made up of history and law. The law was the all-important matter. "The Law" meant this large scroll.

The Prophets. This division was thought of as having two parts: the Former Prophets and the Latter Prophets. The Former Prophets were Joshua, Judges, Samuel, and Kings; i.e., four books. The Latter Prophets were Isaiah, Jeremiah, Ezekiel, and the Twelve; i.e., four books. The Twelve were the twelve small books from Amos to Malachi.

The Writings. These were in four groups. Psalms, Proverbs, and Job made up the first group. Then the Five Scrolls:

Song of Songs, Ruth, Lamentations, Ecclesiastes, and Esther. Next, Daniel. Finally, Ezra, Nehemiah, and Chronicles. In all, eleven books.

According to this arrangement, the Jews counted twenty-four books. This also was the order of the books in Jesus' day. This order should be carefully noted, for it will help us to understand how the Old Testament collection of books grew and gained authority. There is in this arrangement a story in itself. The word "canon" is frequently used for this collection. A "canon" is a rule, so "canon" denotes the accepted books and the order in which they are arranged.

The table of this canon—i.e., the books and their arrangements—should be studied to understand the references in the New Testament to the books of the Old Testament. (See the chart on page 17).

3. JESUS GREW UP IN THE OLD TESTAMENT

The Christian teacher values the Old Testament because it was the book of Jesus' childhood and youth. Much of the story of his early years is in the statement in Luke 4:16, "He went to the synagogue, as his custom was." Place beside this what Luke says in 2:52, "Jesus increased in wisdom." Josephus, a Jew of the first century, wrote: "A Jewish child from the very dawn of undertsanding learned the Law by heart, and had it, as it were, engraved on his soul" (Josephus, Vita 2).

From his earliest days in home and synagogue Jesus heard and memorized the words of the Old Testament. A passage called the *Shema* (Deut. 6:4) was the first to be taught to every child. Jesus also learned the Ten Commandments (Ex. 20:1-17; Deut. 5:6-21). See Mark 10:17-19 and Matthew 22:35-40. Once when a man asked Jesus, "Which commandment is the first of all," Jesus recalled the words of the *Shema* (Deut. 6:4) which he had learned in the synagogue: "Hear, O Israel: The Lord our God, the Lord is one; and you shall love the Lord your God with all your heart, and with all your soul, and with all your mind, and with all your strength" (Mark 12:29). He also recalled Leviticus 19:18, "You shall love your neighbor as yourself." No one else ever put these two commandments together and called them the greatest. But Jesus as he learned these words recognized their supreme importance and had them, so to speak, on the tip of his tongue, ready to answer the question of the scribe. They express the religion of Jesus.

The Old Testament was the curriculum of Jesus' education. His mind became saturated with its words. His thinking was in the statements and ideas of this book. When he was twelve his parents went up to the feast of the Passover, according to the custom. Now that Jesus had become "a son of the law," a responsible young boy instructed in the scriptures, they took him with them. Read Luke 2:41-47. There, in conversation with the teachers, he showed that he had learned the scriptures so that he could listen intelligently, follow a discussion with understanding, answer questions, and ask good questions.

When Jesus came to his baptism and the Holy Spirit came upon him, Jesus heard his Father speaking to him. Read Mark 1:9-11. God speaks in the language and words which fill the mind of the person he addresses. Turn to Psalm 2:7. Jesus had learned this psalm as he grew in wisdom, and now his Father used these words to speak to Jesus as he began his great work: "Thou art my Son." Immediately after this Jesus was sorely tempted (Matt. 4:1-11). In each of the three temptations Jesus met the tempter and overcame him by using scriptures which he had learned in the synagogue. Verses from Deuteronomy (8:3; 6:16; and 6:13) were in his mind as ready weapons with which to wage this fight. So we might go through the words of Jesus down to his last saying on the cross. He expressed the depths of his mind by means of the words lodged there by his strict discipline in the word of God. So the Christian teacher needs to have his mind filled with that very revelation of God which filled the mind of the Master. The Christian teacher needs the Old Testament.

4. JESUS USED THE OLD TESTAMENT IN HIS TEACHING

Read again the story in Luke 4:16-21. When Jesus stood that day in the synagogue where so often he had listened to the reading of the Law and the Prophets and desired to tell his friends and kinsmen about his new work, he read from Isaiah 61:1-2. This scripture expressed just what Jesus proposed to bring to pass. He used the Old Testament as the material of his teaching although he was the most original and most startlingly new teacher who had ever appeared. See Mark 1:22, 27-28.

So it was throughout Jesus' whole ministry. It would be an interesting project to go through the Gospels and list all his quotations from, and references to, the Old Testament. In Luke 24:27 we read, "And beginning with Moses and all the prophets, he interpreted to them in all the scriptures the things concerning himself." Note how much is said in this. Jesus knew the scriptures thoroughly and he knew how to use them in teaching. "He interpreted," that is, he helped his disciples to understand. The Christian teacher should learn to use the Old Testament because the Master Teacher did.

5. THE EARLY CHURCH USED THE OLD TESTAMENT

Here is another important fact: During the earliest days of the church the only scripture in the church was the Old Testament. At the beginning the disciples were Jews and the church was in the city of Jerusalem. The first Christian sermon on record was preached by Peter on the Day of Pentecost. See Acts 2:14-36. In his sermon Peter employed quotations from the Old Testament to prove his claims concerning Jesus. In those days the Septuagint (the Old Testament translated into Greek) was used widely. Jesus himself wrote nothing and it was some time before his followers wrote anything. Therefore the first disciples, Jews trained in the Old Testament, used the Hebrew scriptures. They searched them for material for their preaching and teaching. They referred constantly to the Law and the Prophets. The words which they selected from their old Jewish scriptures formed a part of the message with which they went forth when taking the gospel to the Roman Empire. What is written in the New Testament must be understood in the light of the Old Testament. The Christian teacher must understand the Old Testament if he is to understand the New Testament.

6. THE CHURCH REARRANGED THE BOOKS OF THE OLD TESTAMENT

We have seen how the scriptures were arranged at first (page 12 ff.). But in time, as the church used the Old Testament, certain changes were made in the classification and order of the books. So we have a Christian canon of the Old Testament. This list should be reviewed. It is not easy to keep in mind the names of the thirty-nine books of the Old Testament, or to remember the exact order in which they stand, or to find passages in them quickly. Surely the Christian teacher must at the beginning of this study do some careful work and must improve his memorization of the names of the books.

Review the list as found in the front of the Bible. Go down through the names of the books one by one. Give each name attention, especially the less familiar names.

Take your Bible in hand and go through the Old Testament book by book to note again the names of the books and the order in which they occur. Observe where the books are in your Bible. Consult the table which shows the Christian canon.

Consider how you can help the pupils in your class to gain a fresh and more accurate memorization of this list. Consider how you can have them use their Bibles during the class period. The Christian teacher should know how to find his way around in the book which Jesus studied and used.

THE HEBREW CANON	THE CHRISTIAN CANON
THE LAW Genesis, Exodus, Leviticus, Numbers, Deuteronomy **THE PROPHETS** FORMER PROPHETS: Joshua, Judges, Samuel, Kings LATTER PROPHETS: Isaiah, Jeremiah, Ezekiel, The Twelve **THE WRITINGS** Psalms, Proverbs, Job Song of Songs, Ruth, Lamentations, Ecclesiastes, Esther Daniel Ezra, Nehemiah, Chronicles	**HISTORY** Genesis, Exodus, Leviticus, Numbers, Deuteronomy, Joshua, Judges, Ruth, 1 Samuel, 2 Samuel, 1 Kings, 2 Kings, 1 Chronicles, 2 Chronicles, Ezra, Nehemiah, Esther **POETRY** Job, Psalms, Proverbs, Ecclesiastes, Song of Solomon **MAJOR PROPHETS** Isaiah, Jeremiah (Lamentations), Ezekiel, Daniel **MINOR PROPHETS** Hosea, Joel, Amos, Obadiah, Jonah, Micah, Nahum, Habakkuk, Zephaniah, Haggai, Zechariah, Malachi

2

THE OLD TESTAMENT IS A BOOK OF HISTORY

THE GOD OF THE OLD TESTAMENT is the God of History. He made himself known in a series of events in which he showed himself in his work, carrying out his purpose and revealing his nature by what he did. The Old Testament covers a long period of history—a period sufficiently long to demonstrate clearly God's purpose both by judgment and by deliverance.

One of the primary requirements for understanding and teaching the Old Testament is a knowledge of this history as a whole. This can be grasped by every teacher. Many Christian teachers are acquainted with only a few characters and events which happen to interest them. They do not see the story as a whole; they do not understand each item as a part of a whole. This chapter aims to give the over-all view of the Old Testament as a book of history which sets forth God's mighty acts in their wholeness. The teacher should learn the chief events and characters in their right order; he should see the successive crises of God's judgment and deliverance.

Furthermore, the teacher should learn to give a brief sketch of Hebrew history with the interpretation which gives meaning to it all, according to God's purpose. This whole can be seen and God can become better known by seeing his over-all action in history.

To help teachers in getting started on this comprehensive view, this chapter provides: (1) a survey of the historical books of the Old Testament; (2) a time line for the whole period of the Old Testament; (3) a table of the chief events; (4) a sketch of the whole period; (5) some psalms which recite the mighty acts of God. Each of them and all of them together should enable the teacher to stand at a place where he can view the whole as one views a mountain range or the course of a river.

1. A Survey of the Historical Books of the Old Testament

From Genesis to Esther there are seventeen books to which we may turn to learn the history of the Old Testament period. There is no continuous, complete narrative. There is no chronological record covering this history in regular order, such as is found in a modern textbook on history. But these books begin with creation and reach down to about four hundred years before Christ. These books are in two series.

Genesis through Kings is one series. This series begins with creation and goes as far as the Exile. According to Hebrew thought, it is divided into two parts. Genesis, Exodus, Leviticus, Numbers, and Deuteronomy constitute the Law. These books give the Law in the setting of history. They relate that history which is needed for an understanding of the Law. They give the great events by which the Law is understood. The books, Joshua through Kings, are called the Former Prophets. They set forth God's work in connection with the Hebrew kingdom.

Chronicles, Ezra, and Nehemiah make up the second series. This series begins with Adam and goes down to the time of Ezra and Nehemiah. It is priestly in its interest. It is Temple-centered. History is related only in so far as it concerns the Levitical priesthood and the Temple. At certain points it parallels the first series. Ruth is a short story which fits into the early history. Esther, another short story, belongs to the latest period of the history.

These books are not histories in the strictest sense of the word. They may be called "covenant history" or "redemption history," for they tell about the making and keeping of the covenant and relate God's redemptive action. We cannot, by means of these books, write a full historical account. Although some periods are given fully, others are told sketchily, some are duplicated. But the great events are there, and they show the mighty acts of the covenant-making Redeemer. From other Old Testament books we can learn more about the history, and now archaeology is giving us a great deal of useful background information. So, with all our sources put together, we can know the history of the Hebrew people clearly enough to comprehend God at work in his chosen people for their salvation and the salvation of the whole world.

A preliminary outline will indicate the stages of this history.

Genesis, chaps. 1-11. The beginning of the human race.

Genesis, chaps. 12-50. The choice and training of Abraham and his family to be a blessing to the whole human race.

Exodus, Leviticus, Numbers, Deuteronomy. The call and discipline of the Hebrew tribes, the making of the covenant, and the giving of the Law.

Joshua through Kings. The story of the Hebrews as the chosen people. God's dealing with them through the prophets. The destruction of the sinful kingdom.

Chronicles, Ezra, Nehemiah. The story of the priesthood and the Temple. The destruction of the sinful kingdom. The return from the Exile. The building of the new Temple. The work of Ezra and Nehemiah.

2. A Time Line for the Period of the Old Testament

A time line helps the eye. By it one can see the long spread of time and can place the main events with the characters involved. A full time line is furnished on pages 26-27 of this book. This should be consulted frequently to get a bird's-eye view of the period and to fix it in mind. It should be reviewed for each lesson. An enlarged copy to display before the class will be helpful.

First, note the period of Hebrew history in a simple time line. There is a span of 2000 years. This is a long stretch of time. Many events took place. Many persons were involved. God took time to work out his purpose. God was at work during this whole period in the people whom he had chosen for his purpose.

2000 B.C.	1000 B.C.	B.C.—A.D.

This period divides into two large divisions, two millenniums. The first division, from 2000 B.C. to 1000 B.C., witnessed the beginning of the Hebrew nation. The outstanding names in that period were Abraham and Moses. It took that long to form a people for God's good pleasure. David stands at the point where that period ends and the next period begins. He marks the emergence of the Hebrew kingdom. Ezra, near 400 B.C., marks the beginning of the Jewish community devoted to the study of the Law and trained in the synagogue. When these primary divisions are visualized and these few names are placed, the groundwork for a comprehensive view will be established. This simple time line can be enriched by entering outstanding events and the principal steps in the story.

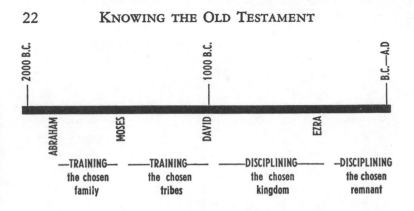

Second, note the great world empires of this period. The Hebrew people were always a comparatively small group. They were placed in the midst of larger powers who fought for world dominion. These empires, strong in numbers and resources, were always threatening the Hebrews or actually ruling over them. The Hebrews knew little continuing independence. For the inhabitants of Palestine there could be no isolation. So the reader of the Old Testament needs to know at every step what empires are playing a part in the history. It is impossible to understand the word of God in those days of old unless one has some awareness of the clash of powers in the period being studied. For this reason, the time line should be filled in with facts regarding the successive world powers.

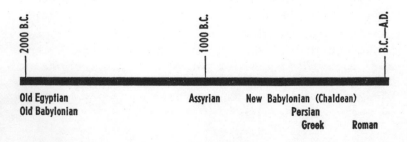

The Old Testament history was full of changes, as can be seen from this table of the nations. New rulers made new conditions and brought new ideas. Life in Palestine never got in a rut. Life was turned upside down time after time. There were also the changes that came with man's new discoveries and inventions. During the period from 2000 to 1000 B.C., the Hebrews lived in the stone and copper age. Their utensils, tools, and weapons were of stone or bronze. See David with his slingshot (1 Sam. 17:40). About 1200 B.C. big changes came in. The use of iron was discovered and the iron age began with new and better utensils, tools, and weapons. In this same era the alphabet was formed and this new means of communication was introduced. Camels were first domesticated as means of rapid transit on the desert, making a new day in trade and war. Horses and chariots were introduced into Palestine. When David became king, a new age was opening in Palestine and the land saw a prosperity unknown before.

Take a brief look at Old Testament history in the light of these facts. The Hebrews (Abraham and his family) appeared as a migrant family in the period of the Old Babylonian and Egyptian empires. There was a disturbance in those empires in that period and many tribes and peoples were on the move. Invasions of nomad tribes poured into the old civilizations. The Hebrews were a part of this pioneering movement. They attempted to settle in Canaan, but finally established themselves on the eastern border of Egypt. Later the children of Abraham, Isaac, and Jacob, a federation of tribes, escaped from Egypt. They moved about as migrant tribes in the desert and then invaded Canaan. Here they spread over the land as shepherds and farmers, living partly as nomads in tents and partly as farmers in small villages—a people of the stone and copper age.

Living by tribes, they tended toward clannishness. They
fought with one another and united only when hard pressed
by foes. Tribes disregarded other tribes when the danger
was remote, but got together occasionally when confronted
by a common danger. Step by step they were forced toward
union, and finally, they were organized into a kingdom. In
the period from about 1200 to 900 B.C., no empire was
strong enough to rule in Palestine. This gave to David and
Solomon the opportunity to make a strong Hebrew kingdom which dominated the whole of Palestine and was able
to continue for about 500 years.

Assyria, however, regained her strength by developing
greater military power in the iron age. Palestine was invaded time after time. After many ups and downs which
kept the Hebrew kingdom in constant trouble, the Assyrians
became the dominant world power. In 722 B.C. they destroyed the Northern Kingdom and made the Southern
Kingdom a small, weak vassal. Assyria fell in 612 B.C. The
new Babylonian or Chaldean Empire took control. Nebuchadnezzar destroyed the Hebrew kingdom in 586 B.C.
and carried the most important part of the Hebrews into
exile. In 539 B.C. the Persians under Cyrus established
themselves as the rulers of the world.

Persia brought a new day. Now we enter "Jewish" history—that is, the history of the Hebrews who made up the
tribe of Judah. The Jewish community in Jerusalem was
reactivated. But now the Jews had no king. From this point
on we have the Jewish church, a religious community with
no political power. In time these arose one of the greatest
characters of the whole story, Ezra. He gathered the books
of the Law together and made of the Jewish people a nation
devoted to the study and observance of the Law. By 333
B.C. the Jews were brought under the control of Greek
masters, beginning with Alexander the Great. In 63 B.C.

Rome became the master of this chosen people. In this era the Jews were scattered over the whole world. Everywhere they went they established the synagogue; they studied, observed, and taught the Law, and so became a light to the nations.

Thus, looking over the length of the time line, we see a history marked by many great changes. The reader needs to sense these different conditions and varying circumstances.

3. The Great Events of Old Testament History

The Old Testament story of God at work in his chosen people is marked by certain outstanding events. This time line gives, as it were, a long range of mountains. There appear on this profile certain prominent peaks and certain deep valleys. These need to be carefully marked. The following table will help in getting the outstanding events in mind. If these are learned in their right order at this stage of the study, they will serve to keep these events in right relationship to one another and to indicate how God used crisis after crisis to make himself known to his people with deepening understanding. God's lesson had to be learned by Israel in the processes of history, in the hard school of experience, in the slow, oft-repeated hard knocks of tragedy. In learning this list the pupil should keep himself responsive to God at work.

4. A Sketch of the Whole Period of the Old Testament

Now that the materials have been assembled in the time line, the story of the Old Testament can be compressed into a brief sketch which reader, teacher, or pupil can carry in his mind. Christians should be able to tell this story from beginning to end in its main features. The pattern used by news writers is useful in such a sketch. They state the whole

TIME LINE
(Read down)

B.C.	Events		Persons
2000 B.C. / 1900	1. Abraham, in obedience to the divine call, went forth to establish a nation which should become a blessing to the whole world.	Call to become God's chosen people.	Abraham, Sarah
1800			Isaac, Rebekah, Jacob, Joseph
1700			
1600			
1500			
1400	2. Moses, in obedience to the divine call, led his people out of slavery in Egypt and bound them to God by the covenant at the mountain of God.	Primary tragedy and redemption. Call to become covenanted nation.	Moses
1300	3. The tribes of Israel invaded Canaan and secured a home.		Joshua
1200			Deborah, Gideon
1100	4. Under Saul and David the Kingdom was established.		Samuel, Saul, David

Date	Persons	Theme	Events
1000	Solomon Rehoboam Jeroboam I		5. Because of the tyranny of Solomon and his son Rehoboam, the kingdom was divided.
900	Elijah Ahab		6. Elijah began the movement of the great prophets.
800	Jeroboam II Amos Hosea Isaiah Micah		7. The Northern Kingdom was destroyed by the Assyrians, 722 B.C.
700	Josiah Jeremiah		
600	Ezekiel	Second tragedy and redemption. Call to become light to the Gentiles.	8. The Southern Kingdom was destroyed by the Babylonians, 586 B.C. 9. A New Start was made in Jerusalem under the persians, 538 B.C.
500	Ezra Nehemiah		10. Ezra bound the nation to the study and observance of the Law.
400			
300			
200	Judas Maccabeus	Third tragedy and redemption.	11. Persecuted by Antiochus Epiphanes, the Jews won their freedom under the Maccabees.
100			"The fulness of the time."
Anno Domini			12. Jerusalem was destroyed by the Romans and the Jews were scattered among the nations.

in a compact introductory paragraph and then enlarge this in succeeding paragraphs, so the whole is driven home by condensation and repetition. In the following report of God's acts in history this method is employed.

The Old Testament gives us the story of God at work among a particular people that they might become the light of all the people of God's creation. The story begins with the creation of man, then goes on to tell how God selected and called one group, the Hebrews, to be a blessing to all the nations. It tells how God disciplined the chosen people in tragedy after tragedy, in punishments and deliverances. The climax comes in God's scattering this disciplined people far and wide with the Law, the Prophets, and the Writings, that they might become a light to all nations. So the day was prepared for the fullness of God's revelation in his Son (Heb. 1:1-2).

This revealing story goes back to the very beginnings of human history, to God's creation of man, for it is the story of the creation of heaven and earth and all that is therein. The story opens with an account of the beginnings of all the families of the earth, and shows how they are interrelated in God's creative act. The story is always of the Creator of all flesh, the Savior of the world. The sin of man and its consequences are emphasized. The tragedy of sin at the beginning of life constitutes the prelude of this story. But God had a purpose for his creation. *Out of* all these peoples and *for* all these peoples, God chose and called Abraham. The story then deals with this man's family.

God trained this family to prepare a people who in turn might serve his purposes for mankind everywhere. Then, through Moses, God called this people out of bondage in Egypt, delivered them in a mighty act at the Red Sea, that they might become a free, chosen people of divine destiny. After making a covenant with them at Sinai, the Mountain of God (a covenant which bound these tribes in a moral obligation whereby he became their God and they became his people), God instructed them in the Law, the fundamental ordinances of a religious community. Through the stern discipline of a generation compelled to live in the desert, God made these people ready to enter into the vigorous life of the land of Canaan, the key geographical setting of the ancient world. At the very crossroads of the nations, these chosen people were thrust into the life of all the nations of the world and then for a thousand years God worked in the drama of national and international tensions.

The story of the Hebrews as a nation began with tribes, a dozen centers of group life with all the usual tendencies toward narrow interests, clannishness, and international strife. By the hard pressure of outside forces and by inspired leaders in the days of the Judges, these tribes were driven together and eventually formed a kingdom that they might hold their own against their rivals. This kingdom passed through a very checkered career for about four hundred years, with ups and downs, achievements and failures, punishments and deliverances, good kings and bad kings. Finally the kingdom was utterly destroyed, Jerusalem was devastated, the Temple was ruined, the people were impoverished, scattered, exiled. No more thorough destruction of a nation could be imagined. God's plan that this chosen nation should become the light of all nations seemed utterly defeated. His people had become a shame and a derision.

After the severe punishment of the Exile, God made a new start. Although the Jews (the small surviving group of the Hebrews) were a completely down-and-out people, guilt-laden and justifiably punished, God called them a second time to be his people and a light to the nations. They had no political power and could expect none. Their land was a desolation. They were in despair. There was no possibility of independnce in the setting of the world empires which dominated the world century after century. No king was allowed among them. But God had a purpose which went back to Abraham and Moses. He called his people to a new service.

God now turned their minds to the Law and the Prophets. Under Ezra he made these Jews a nation of students disciplined in the study and practice of the Law. It was in this period that the books of the Old Testament were gathered and organized into the Law, the Prophets, and the Writings.

It was in this period also that the synagogue emerged, one of the most influential institutions in the history of mankind. This was, in each case, a small congregation, a simple democratic gathering of free men with no controlling priesthood. Men assembled to study the Scriptures and to praise the one true God of all the world. The synagogue was a place of worship and a school of religious discipline. The nation was trained in its services. Wherever the Jew went he organized his life in the synagogue so as to teach adults and children the word of God. To it people of all nations came and learned for the first time that there is one God and only one, without any image, and that this One God is the God of loving-kindness and justice for all peoples and all classes. God called the down-and-out exiles to a new task. Through the Scriptures and the synagogue he made them, in accordance with his original purpose, a blessing to all the families of the earth, a light to the nations, and through them he made ready the conditions for the coming of his Son, Jesus Christ.

5. THE OLD TESTAMENT STORY IN PSALMS

Psalms 104-107 show how the Hebrews recalled their national history. They recited the story as an act of praise to the God of history. This celebration of the glory of God was their way of recalling their past. Their celebrative hymns begin with adoration: "Bless the Lord, O my soul," "O give thanks to the Lord, call on his name," "Praise the Lord," "O give thanks to the Lord, for he is good." Each of these psalms begins with praise and ends with praise. History is sung celebratively to make God's works known among the people; to tell of his wondrous, mighty, saving acts.

These psalms provide the true recital of Old Testament history. The history should be told as the story of God at work manifesting his grace and mercy to the sons of men. Looking over the long stretch of time displayed in the time line, noting its characters and events, its tragedies and redemptions, the believer exclaims: "O give thanks to the Lord, for he is good; for his steadfast love endures forever!"

God creates, God calls, God commands, God judges, God punishes, God saves, God reveals.

3

THE BASIC EVENT IN THE OLD TESTAMENT

THE DELIVERANCE FROM BONDAGE in Egypt and the making of the covenant between God and his chosen people constitute the basic fact of Old Testament history and interpretation. "I am the Lord your God, who brought you out of the land of Egypt, out of the house of bondage" (Ex. 20:2).

This marvelous deliverance with the solemn making of the covenant is like the North Star for guiding the reader of the Old Testament. By this gracious act of salvation and covenant, God made himself known in his true nature: "a God merciful and gracious, slow to anger, and abounding in steadfast love and faithfulness" (Ex. 34:6). The writers of the books of the Old Testament were always looking back to this initial event and truing their thinking by it. The prophets were ever calling the nation to remember this deliverance and to think of God in the light of his mercy and righteousness manifested at the Red Sea and at Sinai. The worship of Israel was the repeated celebration of this marvelous redemption. The ethics of Israel were motivated by the recollection of God's act of justice in Israel's emancipation. The character of God was described as he revealed himself in this definite historical event. "He made known his ways unto Moses, his acts to the people of Israel" (Ps. 103:7).

1. THE STORY OF THE DELIVERANCE STANDS AT THE CENTER OF THE FIRST DIVISION OF THE OLD TESTAMENT

This first division of the Old Testament (and a very important one it is) consists of the Pentateuch, i.e., the five books of the Law. At its core is this basic event, the Deliverance. The following outline emphasizes this fact:

> The Creation and Discipline of the Human Race. Gen. 1-11.
> The Call and Discipline of Abraham and His Family. Gen. 12-50.
> The DELIVERANCE. Ex. 1:1—15:21.
> The COVENANT. Ex. 15:22—23:33.
> The Instruction and Discipline in the Wilderness. Ex. 24:1—Deut. 34:12.

This event is seen standing at the center of the impressive declaration of the mighty works of God as set forth in the Pentateuch. It is a great event preceded by great events and followed by great events. God created the human race; then called Abraham and his family to be a blessing to the whole race. God called the tribes of Israel out of slavery and made them a nation to be a blessing to the whole race. God disciplined this new chosen nation by the severe discipline of life in the wilderness. This whole story has unity. Creation is seen in the light of this gracious act of justice, and this act is seen in the light of creation. Each part of the story helps to interpret the other parts. All are bound together in the great act of redemption. The key event is the deliverance of this chosen people.

2. THE STORY OF THE DELIVERANCE IS A CELEBRATIVE RECITAL

Exodus 1:1—15:21 contains one of the really great stories, great in what it recounts, great in its telling of the mighty act, great in its influence wherever the Bible has gone. It is a celebrative story, a dramatic and soul-stirring recital of God at work accomplishing his purpose. All the dynamic power of a song of emancipation can be felt in it. It is written to be recited in the dramatic setting of the yearly reliving of this deliverance as it is cerebrated in the Passover ceremony, that the people of God might feel anew the amazing grace of God. So the story should be read and recited with sympathetic responsiveness to the feelings of the people as they experienced these strange, bitter, surprising, blessed acts of God.

The reader should listen that he may hear the cry of these slaves in the agonies of their oppression. He should feel the compassion of God as he looks upon their misery. "The people of Israel groaned under their bondage, and cried out for help, and their cry under bondage came up to God. And God heard their groaning, and God remembered this covenant with Abraham, with Isaac, and with Jacob. And God saw the people of Israel, and God knew their condition" (Ex. 2:23-25). "Then the Lord said, 'I have seen the affliction of my people who are in Egypt, and have heard their cry because of their taskmasters; I know their sufferings, and I have come down to deliver them . . .' " (Ex. 3:7-8). What tragic pathos and what divine compassion! The reader reads aright only when he enters into the human suffering and the divine pity.

Turn to the last words of the recital to sense these strong feelings: "Sing to the Lord, for he has triumphed gloriously; the horse and his rider he has thrown into the sea" (Ex. 15:21). Joyful celebration: tragic sorrow turned into an outburst of joy; bitter slavery followed by surprising deliverance! Over all the sorrow and joy stands the amazing loving-kindness of God, the Savior. Such is the vibrant song of a people celebrating their deliverance and gladly acknowledging the power and grace of their God. Read Ex. 15:19-

21 with imaginative entrance into the experience of those who were so strangely delivered. Hear Miriam as she takes a timbrel (a tambourine) in hand to lead the celebrative singing. Hear all the women as they join her with their timbrels. See them as they dance in their celebration of emancipation. Exodus 1:1—15:21 is the dynamic recital of the greatest event in the history of this people.

Through the story there runs a solemn note crowded with emotion. "Let my people go" (Ex. 5:1; 8:1; 9:1; 9:13; 10:3). It sounds like the tolling of a bell. Warning to Pharaoh and promise to Israel can be heard in it. God speaks the warning and proclaims the promise. In each case it is a full-toned word of the Lord to be repeated with all its solemnity. The story is to be read with deep emotion. Many questions spring up in the mind of the modern reader asking for explanations. At the outset, these questions should be set aside while the reader enters into the experiences of these people as they pass from bitter bondage into a glorious deliverance. In their immediate experience of these strange events, they had the vivid realization that God saw their plight, heard their cry, visited them in their woe, and delivered them. "Blessed be the name of the Lord!" All these feelings were awakened each Passover as the people by means of this story celebrated again the goodness of God.

3. THE SERIES OF EPISODES IN THE GREAT EVENT

After exposing oneself to the deep feelings of this celebrative story, the whole should be reviewed to get its parts in order. Exodus opens (1:1-7) with the statement that the children of Israel were a fruitful, multiplying, mighty people. The miserable slaves are lifted up into their significance under God. This joyful assertion sets the tone of the story and prepares one to enter into the blessed future about to come to this people.

Exodus 1:8-22 relates their afflictions. Theirs was that bitter suffering known the world over in generation after generation when men of power exploit their victims. Pharaoh was an absolute monarch whose rule was tyrannical and oppressive. In their bitter slavery there was one sustaining strength: God's covenant with Abraham, Isaac, and Jacob. Exodus 2:1—4:31 presents the story of God's raising up his new leader, Moses. In the face of a seemingly impossible situation, God called this man, trained him for his task, and then brought him to Israel to serve the people in their deliverance. Exodus 5:1—11:10 recounts the long contest between Moses and Pharaoh.

These two representatives of opposing forces face each other in this momentous clash. Justice confronted injustice. The God of justice made demands upon the king of injustice. This was a crisis in which all later history was involved. Time after time the cause of righteousness seemed lost. The slaves repeatedly got the worst of it. Tyranny is never willing to give in. The tyrant refuses to change his mind.

In this struggle a law of God is seen. "The Lord hardened the heart of Pharaoh" (Ex. 9:12; see also 4:21; 10:20, 27; 11:10; 14:4, 8, 17). It is God's law that when a tyrant refuses to hear the cry of oppressed people, he becomes harder and harder of heart. When he suppresses his tender feelings, he destroys those tender feelings. When he refuses to act mercifully, he becomes one without mercy. His inner nature is toughened. This is a solemn law of God's moral rule. But God has his way in such a struggle. He can use the calamities of nature so that they become plagues to the wicked and blessing to the faithful. So God used the plagues in the valley of the Nile and so he used the east wind at the Red Sea.

Finally there is the escape at the Red Sea (Ex. 12:1—14:30). How dreadful the scene! The solemn observance of the Passover, the death of the first-born of the Egyptians, the hurried escape by night, the flight toward the border, the pursuit by Pharaoh's army, the seeming defeat for Israel. In spite of Moses' promises, the people seemed trapped and doomed. Little wonder that they cried out in despair and shouted against Moses.

Then the miracle. The surprise of surprises. An east wind blew back the waters at the head of the gulf of the Red Sea ("Sea of Reeds," according to the Hebrew) and Israel passed over into freedom, while the Egyptian forces were caught and drowned when the waters flowed back again! It is difficult for us to feel to the full the emotions of Israel at that moment. The Hebrews could never forget that surprising, amazing, unheard-of deliverance. Then Moses and the people sang this song to the Lord:

"I will sing to the Lord, for he has triumphed gloriously;
   the horse and his rider he has thrown into the sea.
The Lord is my strength and my song,
   and he has become my salvation" (Ex. 15:1-2).

4. THE MAKING OF THE COVENANT (Ex. 15:22—23:33)

After the excitement of the deliverance, the people of Israel were led by Moses into the wilderness. There they faced the severe hardships of thirst and hunger in the waterless, unproductive desert. At times they cursed Moses as they longed for their gardens in Egypt. But eventually Moses brought them to the Mountain of God, called Sinai or Horeb. There the covenant between God and Israel was made.

The religion of the Bible is a covenant religion. There are two covenants or testaments: the old covenant and the new covenant; i.e., the Old Testament and the New Testament. This gives to our religion a definite quality and nature which makes it different from all other religions. So it is of the utmost importance that the reader of the Old Testament understand the meaning of a covenant and of this particular covenant at the Mountain of God. A covenant is a solemn, binding agreement between two parties. Each member is under sacred obligation. Each party binds himself to the other party by sworn promises. To break a covenant brings a person under severest judgment and punishment. The covenant is stated in the terms of this solemn mutual obligation: "I will be their God, and they shall be my people" (Jer. 31:33). The Israelites had been delivered from bondage; now thy must enter into a binding covenant with their deliverer.

Moses led the people to Mt. Sinai, the Mountain of God. The making of such a covenant needed an impressive setting that it might work deep into the minds of all the people. Mt. Sinai furnished such a setting. One is to imagine the lofty, craggy mountain with clouds about its top and storms displaying their awesome power. About the foot of the mountain the people were gathered. A line was fixed beyond which no person was to pass. The "Holy" to these people was a dreadful, dangerous power threatening death to those who were not prepared to approach the sacred area. Moses went to the top of the mountain to commune with God while the people tarried at the foot. There was a special holiness in that mountain and Moses had a special holiness.

Then there was the sacrifice. On an altar animals were offered. The blood of the sacrificed animals was the sacred element. By the blood, the covenant-making was made sacred, a life-commitment. The slaying of the animals and the sprinkling of the blood became the solemn symbols by which the covenant was made a holy, moral, lasting obligation.

The account of the events at Sinai is complicated because there is an intermixing of events and laws. The story of the events, however, can be easily followed by reading the passages in the following order:

The Journey to Sinai. Ex. 15:22—18:27.
The Making of the Covenant. Ex. 19:1-25; 24:1-18; 32:1-34; 35.
The Laws of the Covenant. Ex. 25:1—31:18; 35:1—40:38.

These passages tell of the gathering of the people at the foot of the Mountain of God, of Moses going to the top of the mountain to receive the Law, and of his bringing the Law to the people and binding them under the covenant.

5. THE TEN COMMANDMENTS (Ex. 20:1-17; Deut. 5:6-21)

The Law of the Covenant is compressed into the Ten Commandments. There are many laws in the Book of Exodus, including the elaborate instructions regarding the Tabernacle, but the heart of the legislation is contained in this Decalogue.

The introductory statement is the key to these laws. It should be read with the ten laws to give them proper explanation. "I am the Lord your God, who brought you out of the land of Egypt, out of the house of bondage" (Ex. 20:1; Deut. 5:6). First, the great event is stated. God's gracious act of deliverance is recalled. The people are to observe these laws because God has become their Deliverer, Savior, Redeemer. The strongest motive is placed back of these laws. This shows again how the deliverance from bondage is the key event for understanding the Old Testament.

These ten laws do not cover everything, but they give fundamental rules for the people of the covenant, rules which go to the heart of the moral law. They are basic rules for the people of God, whereby they may live in right relation with God and with one another. But in reading the Ten Commandments, emphasis should always be placed on the opening words, "I am the Lord your God, who brought you out of the land of Egypt, out of the house of bondage." This statement gives the interpretation and motivation of the laws. It is the essential, indispensable introduction. Only with this introduction does the recital of the Decalogue properly begin.

6. GOD'S NAME (Ex. 3:1-22; 6:1-13)

The third chapter of Exodus recounts that experience in the life of Moses in which there was made known to him the Name of the God of Israel. This moment of God's revelation brings us to the very heart of the great event. Moses had spent many years as a keeper of flocks in the wilderness. This was a long discipline in thinking, the discipline of a deeply searching mind profoundly concerned with his people and feeling mightily God's concern for them. All his thoughts were directed toward his brothers (Ex. 2:11). Moses had seen their afflictions. Their cry rang in his soul. God's mind was at work in Moses' mind. Moses' burning desire was to deliver his people from bondage and bring them into a goodly land. Now the time seemed at hand.

Moses moved his flocks to "the backside of the desert" (KJV). That is, to the west side, toward the land where his people were in bitter bondage. There God confronted Moses in one of the deepest experiences man has ever known. A strange fire burned in the bush; a strange fire burned in Moses' heart. God was in the strange fire outside and in the strange fire inside. The Presence both outside and within made this a profound meeting with God. Moses was ordained by fire. He became the Man of God, the Leader of Israel.

In this fiery commissioning there arose a question, "What is God's name?" What name should Moses use in speaking of God to Israel? In that day that was a necessary question, for it was a time of many gods and many names. Each people had a god of its own. And there were many gods for various functions in life. The word "god" (*elohim* in Hebrew) was a general word with no individual meaning. Each god had to have a name. Moses could not say to his people, "God sent me." That would not be clear to them. So Moses inquired of the Presence at the burning bush, "If they ask me, 'What is his name?' what shall I say to them?"

The reader and teacher of the Old Testament needs to give careful attention to understand the Name. See Exodus 6:2: "And God said to Moses, 'I am the LORD. I appeared to Abraham, to Isaac, and to Jacob, as God Almighty, but by my name the LORD I did not make myself known to them.'" "God Almighty" is the translation of two Hebrew words, *El Shaddai*. Now turn to the King James Version. The last part of this verse reads, "But by my name JEHOVAH was I not known to them." (See also the American Standard Version of 1901.) Why these two ways of translation? In the Hebrew we find at this place four consonants, YHWH. In the Jewish scriptures they kept this form, "My name YHWH." This form in time became a sacred word which was not spelled out and which was not pronounced. The Jews, when they read the scriptures, used instead their word for "lord," *adonai*. The church followed the Jewish custom. The Greeks used their word for "lord," *Kyrios;* the Romans used *Dominus;* the Germans, *Herr;* the English, *Lord*. But "Lord" is not a name and it is not a translation of YHWH. In the Middle Ages someone invented a new word. He attached the vowels of the Hebrew word for "lord" to these four consonants and contrived the artificial form, "Jehovah." This is not a form known in

Hebrew, but it now has been used so much that it has become a well-known name. "Jehovah" is found four times in the King James Version. "My name JEHOVAH" (Ex. 6:3). "That men may know that thou, whose name alone is JEHOVAH, art the most high over all the earth" (Ps. 83:18). "The Lord JEHOVAH is my strength and my song" (Isa. 12:2). "In the LORD JEHOVAH is everlasting strength" (Isa. 26:4). In all other places where YHWH occurs, the King James Version used "Lord." English readers are accustomed to this form and naturally prefer it.

Jehovah, accordingly, is not a Hebrew word and was not the form used by Moses. What, then, was the name given to Moses at the Burning Bush? What was the name which he used in speaking to the Hebrew tribes? YHWH, when given the proper vowels, is YaHWeH. "Yahweh" is his name, and this name is used constantly in the Old Testament. "Lord" is not a name but a title. "Yahweh" is a name, the designation of an individual. Exodus 6:3, correctly translated, reads: "But by my name Yahweh I did not make myself known to them." Exodus 3:16, literally translated, reads: "Go and gather the elders of Israel together and say to them: 'Yahweh, the God of your fathers, the God of Abraham, of Isaac, and of Jacob, has appeared unto me, saying. . . .'" In Exodus 3:18, Moses is bidden to say to Pharaoh, "Yahweh, the God of the Hebrews, has met with us; and now, we pray you, let us go a three days' journey into the wilderness, that we may sacrifice to Yahweh, our God." The Hebrews needed a distinct, individual name to identify their God, as utterly different from all other gods. This is one of the unique features of the Old Testament. See Isaiah 42:8: "I am Yahweh, that is my name." "Yahweh, the god of Israel." "Yahweh, our God." "Thus says Yahweh." These are frequent expressions. When all the other so-called gods became nonentities to the Hebrews, they no longer needed an individual name for the One and Only God," so they used their word for "Lord" where YHWH is written. The church has followed this custom. In the Revised Standard Version, "Lord" is used consistently, but Jehovah or Yahweh is indicated in the footnotes. (See the Preface of the Revised Standard Version, pages vi and vii in the 1952 edition.)

In Exodus 3:14 there is another answer to Moses' question. "God said to Moses, 'I AM WHO I AM.' And he said, 'Say this to the people of Israel, "I AM" has sent me to you.' " This, as can be seen by consulting the footnote for this passage, may be read, "I AM WHAT I AM" or "I WILL BE WHAT I WILL BE." The connection between "Yahweh" and "I am" is not clear to the English reader. In Hebrew the verb "be" (am) and the form "Yahweh" are from the same root. "I am" and "Yahweh" contain the same basic meaning. "I am" refers to God's presence. "I am" equals "I am present, I am here." It is a word of assurance. In their suffering God seemed afar off. But Moses is commissioned to declare God's presence, God's activity, God's redeeming activity. The psalmist sings, "God is our refuge and strength, a very present help in trouble" (Ps. 46:1). That gives the idea in this word of assurance, "I AM WHO I AM." Israel can count on God. "I am who I am *in your affliction. I will be who I will be in your deliverance.*" The name "Yahweh" was made full of meaning for Israel by his delivering them from bondage and making his covenant with them. He showed himself the God of loving-kindness, steadfast love, covenant constancy, justice, righteousness; the Redeemer. "I am" included all this.

The Great Event brought to Israel a new name for God, a new name by which God could reveal himself, a new name by which Israel could speak to God. Every time "Yahweh," "Jehovah," or "the Lord" is used in the Old

Testament, the name must be filled with all the meaning that comes from God's mighty and gracious act in redeeming Israel.

Turn to Psalm 27 to get the feeling for and understanding of this name "Yahweh." Wherever "Lord" occurs in the English translation, read "Yahweh" as in the original and sense the meaning of this name as used in the fervent praises of Israel. Join with Israel in magnifying his name and in calling upon his name.

4

UNITY AND VARIETY

THIRTY-NINE BOOKS which make one book! The Old Testament is remarkable for both its variety and its unity. In its parts there are many differences; in its entirety there is distinct oneness. This makes the Old Testament a very rich and interesting book.

In reading the Old Testament, one always makes fresh and surprising discoveries. The unity is not sameness, repeated time after time. The Old Testament never lacks originality and individuality in its parts, as though its parts were cut from the same pattern. There is the variety which is always found in life, for it is the living word. "Thy word is like a garden, Lord." This garden of the Lord has many flowers bright and fair with their many delightful varieties. But the garden as a whole has a pattern and character given it by the Gardener. So the Old Testament has unity in God himself.

The Old Testament does not give a fixed system of thought, but confronts us with the one true God, the same in all the different times, persons, and literary forms of his revelation. To learn to appreciate the rich variety and at the same time the living oneness is a privilege of the student of the Old Testament. In this chapter we shall look first at the variety and second at the unity. Both may be easily discerned.

1. The Variety in the Old Testament

This book is as wide and many sided as human life. There is no kind of circumstance, no kind of person, no kind of writing that is not found in the Old Testament. The whole range of human feelings is lived out in its account of life, so that it has something for each reader pertinent to what that reader is experiencing. There is no problem or hope, no sorrow or joy, which was not known in the actualities of life by some character in these many writings. In reading, one should not think of a mere chronicle of happenings of long ago, remote from the reader's life, but should read with quickened sensitivity to the very real experiences of people like oneself. One should read, weeping with those who despair and shouting for joy with those who celebrate the goodness of God. Yes, lamenting with those who lament and joining the Hallelujahs of those who sing the new song of redemption.

(a) The Variety of Times and Circumstances. Review the time line. From 2000 B.C. down to the close of the Old Testament, how varied were the outward circumstances of life! In passing from the stone and bronze age into the iron age, ancient peoples experienced many changes in the utensils of daily life and in the means of commerce with more distant places. To get copper and iron was very important. The trade in these metals determined prosperity. Solomon was able to grow in riches and power because he controlled the iron mines and iron smelting of Akaba, and also the trade in horses and chariots between the faraway lands of the Egyptians and the Hittites. The work of archaeology has shown how the life of cities changed as men advanced in the iron age.

How different the modes of living in this long stretch of time! Abraham and his family were nomads who wandered about slowly with their flocks over the wide areas from Mesopotamia to Egypt. We must visit Abraham at his tent, experience his hospitality, walk with him in the brilliantly starred glory of the Palestinian night, stand with him by his simple altar of a few field stones, and in the sacrifice of an animal renew the covenant with God Almighty. How changed the life of his descendants as they lived on the eastern border of Egypt tending herds, making their gardens, toiling under their taskmasters! There followed century after century, alteration succeeding alteration. The days of hunger and thirst, hope and fear, in the hardships of the desert; the period of the Judges, living as immigrant tribes, winning and making a homeland for themselves; the time of the kings and empires, with all the vicissitudes, prosperities and depressions, of internal and external conflict; the sad, lamentable years of the Exile when everything was destroyed and they were like a valley of dead bones; the thrilling new day when they marched out of Babylon and returned to the promised land; the long period during which they were a small, poor, economically afflicted people under the mighty world empires; the new life in the synagogue devoted to the study of the Law; the dispersion throughout the world, a peculiar, separate people witnessing to the worship of one imageless, moral God in the midst of pagan polytheism.

How different the needs and moods of these people, in these long changing centuries in which they touched the whole range of human experience! There is nothing of the ups-and-downs of life which the writers of the Old Testament did not taste in all its bitterness or joy. The universal appeal of the Old Testament comes from this wide range of time. A book by one man written in one situation could never have touched life at so many different points.

(b) **The Variety of Persons.** Every type of individual appears in this long history. They are many, and many of their names are familiar. Many of their stories are among the best known. Here is a list of twenty-five:

David, Deborah, Ezra, Amos, Sarah, Isaiah, Joshua, Abraham, Joseph, Jeroboam, Nathan, Nehemiah, Isaac, Gideon, Jeremiah, Rebecca, Jacob, Solomon, Ahab, Adam, Moses, Elijah, Saul, Ezekiel, Noah.

Try putting these names in their historical order, for each should be understood in the light of his or her own day. Arranging them in their right order and placing them on a time line is a good exercise. They were real persons. Each had distinctive qualities, temperaments, abilities, and limitations. Each was molded by certain circumstances. One of the features of true Bible study is the exercise of becoming acquainted with each of these Bible persons in his own character.

Too frequently these men and women are vaguely characterized by the simple description, "good" or "bad." But one should learn to go beyond abstract words and be able to give a distinct description of an individual. For example, one must see David as a warrior king, an ambitious, popular leader full of the contradictions of a warm-hearted, vital builder of a new kingdom, living in the ethics of warfare and polygamy. How different was Ezra in a day when there could be no kingdom, a quiet, diligent student copying out the Law and teaching his people! How different the parts they played in the work of God! David must be known in his time and character; Ezra in his. David was good for his task. Ezra was good for his assignment. Both the persons and the circumstances differed.

It took many persons of many gifts to make God known. God spoke to a wide variety of men and women in many ways and many portions (Heb. 1:1). Ruth was a simple village girl in the pattern of life of ancient Moab and Bethlehem; Esther was a member of the harem of a Persian monarch. Gideon was a clever man of war, a tribal chief in days of tribal rivalry; Jeremiah was a saintly pursuer of the deep, inner life in a day of international upset. Nathan made a good start as a prophet, but got mixed up in a palace intrigue; Isaiah detached himself from court politics and lived a long life as the critic of kings and the instructor of a small band of disciples. Each person should be seen in his distinct individuality and in his particular life situation.

Amos, Hosea, Micah, and Isaiah were prophets in the same period, but each, as we shall see, was a distinct type of person. God's call to each of these men was in accordance with that individual's temperament. Contrast Jonah, Jeremiah, and Isaiah. Jonah attempted to flee from God's call and had to pass through a catastrophe to be made a prophet. Jeremiah timidly shrank from his call and had to be built up in inner strength for his severe task. Isaiah responded spontaneously with prompt acceptance, "Here am I, send me." Such was the variety of temperaments.

How God worked in and through each individual in his given situation is the important fact to know. God used Gideon and his gifts at a certain time. Gideon is not a model character to be copied, for none other is placed in his position. God used David and his gifts at a particular time in Hebrew history, but in another crisis he needed a very different type, as we have noted in Ezra. To understand these man and to use their stories calls for a disciplined imagination which can enter into each type of character and see the times in which he lived. We do not have stories of model characters. The story of David is very frank. This clever activist in the situation of a rising king, in a warlike, polygamous era, is never prettified or made saintly. But God was at work in this man in this situation. That is what should be seen clearly. And so with the wide variety. Think of some of them: the daring, adventurous dreamer, Abraham; the quiet, retiring Isaac; the scheming, sensitive, affectionate Jacob; the impulsive, cruel Esau; the conceited, ambitious, able Joseph; the proud, haughty Sarah; the scheming, domineering Rebekah. What variety in just this one family!

(c) **Varieties of Types of Literature.** Many different forms of literature enrich the Old Testament. Songs are prominent throughout the whole book. Songs are one of the earliest and most prevailing methods of human expression. Men sang before they wrote, and songs continue on without ever being put to paper and ink. See such an early, spontaneous rhyme as the Song of the Well in Numbers 21:16-18. There are references to a Book of the Wars of the Lord (Num. 21:14-15) and a Book of Jasher (2 Sam. 1:17-27). In this passage David shows himself to be a skillful composer and singer of a ballad. In Judges 9:7-15 Jotham chanted a very effective fable. In Isaiah 5:1-7 we find a true parable given as a song. What a variety of songs these are! War songs: Numbers 21:14-15; Psalm 18:31-42. Taunt songs: Isaiah 37:21-29; 47:1-15. Laments: Lamentations 1:1-22. Funeral dirges: Amos 5:1-2. The New Song of Redemption: Psalms 96, 98; Isaiah 52: 7-12. The majestic Hymn of Creation: Genesis, chap. 1.

The story is another early and abiding variety of communication. The Old Testament abounds in stories of many kinds, and these are told with real art. The accounts of Abraham and his family, of the Judges and their fighting, and of David and his exploits are enduring examples of this art. There are excellent short stories and powerfully told longer stories. The record of Joseph (Genesis, chaps. 37-50) meets all the requirements of a novelette. Ruth is a model for a short story. The account in 2 Samuel of David and his affairs in family and court is one of the very best pieces of historical narrative in all literature. The Old Testament has a great story to tell, one which produced great storytelling.

Prose writing appears in many varieties. In Exodus, Leviticus, and Deuteronomy there are blocks of codes stated in the proper legal manner. In Ezra, chaps. 1 and 6, the Persia Edict is given in its two customary forms, the one for the court archives, the other for the public proclamation.

In Exodus, chaps. 25-31, there are detailed specifications for the Tabernacle and in 1 Kings 7:1-51 for the Temple. Ezekiel, chaps. 40-48, also displays the prose of the architect. At the courts, records were kept, and there are frequent references to these records (1 Kings 11:41; 14:19, 29; etc.). Family trees often appear with their distinct form of composition. Although not interesting reading, they have a certain impressiveness, especially for establishing a person's status among royalty or the priesthood.

And sermons! The words of the prophets were addressed to public audiences. Their sermons were aimed to change the minds of the listeners. This required the special powers of dealing with audiences, skill in stating the truth, eloquence, and persuasion. All the prophets were poets. Their poetry contains a great deal of dramatic dialogue, for they brought their audiences into direct contact with God. Such speech is full of the changes of mood characteristic of lively contact between speaker and hearers.

Each of these types of literature must be studied and interpreted according to its own genius and use. They are the different tools in the hands of the Creator. One situation called for a fable, another for a sermon; one for a song, another for a story. Each type was so fitted to the situation and so expressed the person of the speaker that we cannot enter into the occasion except by this particular means of expression. We understand the speaker and the situation when we sing the song or actually tell the fable. Again let it be said, we must weep with those who weep and rejoice with those who rejoice. To stand with Isaiah in the face of the threat of Sennacherib and join with him in his taunt song will carry us into that situation; it will take us into the mind of Isaiah and into the mind of God (Isa. 37:21-29).

(d) **The Variety of Kinds of Books.** We count thirty-nine books in the Old Testament. How many distinct kinds of books are there in this collection? Observe certain contrasts. Compare Psalms and Proverbs. The first is made up of hymns and prayers which the Israelites used in their worship. The second is a collection of wise, witty, practical sayings about all sorts of common things in life; it praises the virtue of wisdom. Compare Esther and Job. The first is a popular, naturalistic short story dealing with court intrigues. It does not mention God. The second is a profound drama dealing with man's deepest problems in his relations with God. Compare the Song of Songs with Leviticus. The first is a beautiful, frank love song, celebrating the joy and faithfulness of the true love of two young people. The second is a detailed code for the priests in their solemn services in the Temple. Compare Ecclesiastes and Isaiah. The first is a philosophic meditation on the vanity of life. The second is the great evangel of the Old Testament, overflowing with exuberant faith and great expectations.

These varieties constitute the abundance of the riches of the Old Testament revelation. They show the miraculous versatility of God. To appropriate these riches we must enter into this versatility. A fable must be understood and interpreted as a fable, a ballad as a ballad, an ordinance as an ordinance, a genealogical table as a genealogical table, a dream as a dream, a sermon as a sermon. God's range of approach to the people of long ago and to modern man is as wide as the gamut of his versatility and of our human variations. Studying the Old Testament with this appreciation, the mind is enlarged by a wider sensitivity and susceptibility to God's revelation of himself.

2. THE UNITY OF THE OLD TESTAMENT

The unifier is God himself. The unity of the Old Testament is greater than any uniformity of human planning. The thirty-nine books are not like a line of prefabricated houses. There is an inner unity, rather than an outward sameness. This is realized in the One Person who speaks and acts in all the variety. The binding factor is not in some prescribed doctrine. It is not in any legal statement. The inner, vital, abiding oneness is in the pervading presence of God who operates in all the differences of time and form. What Paul says of the church may be adapted to the Old Testament: "Now there are varieties of gifts, but the same Spirit; and there are varieties of service, but the same Lord; and there are varieties of working, but it is the same God who inspires them all in every one" (1 Cor. 12:4-6). This vital unity can be seen in the following passages.

(a) **Deuteronomy 6:4-9.** This passage is called the *Shema.* This is the Hebrew word for "Hear," the first word in this commandment. The *Shema* is Axiom Number One in Hebrew thought, and therefore it is Lesson Number One in Hebrew instruction. At the very outset of religious education the *Shema* is planted in the memory. This commandment calls for the exclusive worship of one God with all one's faculties. "With all your heart, with all your soul, and with all your might." Compare Psalm 103:1:

"Bless the Lord, O my soul; and all that is within me, bless his holy name." This concentration of the whole of the worshiper—his thoughts, affection, and will—upon one and only one object of worship gives religion a positive focus, a unifying force. In the midst of the common polytheism of the ancient world, the multitude of idols, the low-grade character of the gods, the demand that a people should be completely exclusive in their worship was a very strange requirement. The *Shema* gave to the Hebrews a concentrating power which brought everything into unity.

The Old Testament gave to the world the declaration that there is one God. We call this monotheism. This is a philosophic term which we use when talking about God. The *Shema* brings the worshiper into direct, intimate relation with the One who calls for and deserves the complete loyalty of man's whole being. This is dynamic religion. The living God of the Old Testament is the unifier. Out of this dynamic relationship there came in time the doctrine of One God. First the vital experience of the *Shema;* then the doctrine.

(b) **Psalm 118.** This psalm expresses the true praise of Israel. The first four verses and the last are in a definite form. The first line in each of these verses calls upon the worshiper to praise his God. The second lines are antiphonal responses. A leader in the Temple choirs or in the synagogue pronounced the first lines and the congregation responded with the refrain. This refrain contains a key word. In Hebrew it is HESED. It is rendered in different ways:

"His *mercy* endureth for ever" (King James Version).

"His *lovingkindness* endureth forever" (American Standard Version).

"His *steadfast love* endures for ever" (Revised Standard Version).

In other places, this word is rendered "goodness." Each of these ways of translating it is good. In fact, we need all these English words—goodness, mercy, loving-kindness, steadfast love—to help us understand the meaning of HESED. The basic quality of God in the Old Testament is gracious, merciful, steadfast love. This is what Israel discovered in the great event of the deliverance from bondage. This is what Israel discovered in the deliverance from the Exile. They found in the God of Israel goodness, mercy, loving-kindness, steadfast love, and they sang praises to God because of this. Let it be stated here, and repeated again and again, that it is heresy to say that in the Old Testament there is a God of Wrath and that in the New Testament there is a God of Love. There is one God through both Testaments. In the Old Testament the great word is HESED (loving-kindness); in the New Testament the great word is AGAPE (gracious love). The repeated refrain in Psalm 118:1-4, 29 declares that God's HESED endures forever. In the Hebrew the expression is simply "His HESED forever." That is, it is constant, never failing. God is always, at all times, in all circumstances, good to Israel; God is always merciful, kind, loving, and steadfast. In this lies the unity of the Old Testament. There may be variety of all kinds, but there is one enduring steadfast Person in all and through all—God Himself in his steadfast love.

(c) **Psalm 136.** This is called the Great Hallel, that is, the Great Song of Praise. "Hallel" is the word from which "Hallelujah" comes. So this is a Hallelujah Chorus. Again observe the antiphonal structure. The leader calls upon the people to praise God. In verse after verse he proclaims some specific reason for praise. The congregation responds with the deepest praise possible: "His HESED forever." The leader begins with the simple declaration,

"He is good." In vss. 2-9 the leader exalts God, the Creator. In vss. 10-15 he celebrates God's goodness in the deliverance from bondage. In vss. 16-22 he recounts God's goodness in leading his people through the wilderness and into the Promised Land. In vss. 23-24 he recalls the constant care of God in adversities. Then in vs. 25 God's goodness to every human being is praised, and in vs. 26 God is praised in heaven above. While these tokens of God's gracious goodness are being recited, all the people respond to this loving-kindness in the words of this chant of praise. God's loving-kindness is unfailing, everlasting, constant. It is found everywhere and at all times. As it was in the beginning, is now, and ever shall be!

With this word HESED the word "covenant" should be joined. The Old Testament confronts man with the covenant-making and covenant-keeping God. As has been stated, a covenant is a solemn, binding agreement. Faithfulness is its prime requisite. When God made his covenant with Israel, he gave himself to this covenant with never-failing faithfulness, with enduring loving-kindness, with steadfast love. Israel's faith and hope rested on this abiding security. This word HESED is the primary word for God in the Old Testament. "Wrath" is not a frequent word. But HESED is found everywhere. This gives a unique quality to the unity of the Old Testament. God is the unifier, his enduring, steadfast, gracious goodness is the spiritual fact in all. The God who spoke to the fathers in the prophets by various portions and in various manners was the one God of loving-kindness.

(d) Psalm 103. In this beautiful hymn of praise, so deeply treasured by the church, we find again the heart of the Old Testament experience of God. The supreme, underlying truth is wonderfully expressed in this song of gratitude and consecration. Notice how God is described.

Verse 8 is the key verse: "The Lord is merciful and gracious, slow to anger and abounding in steadfast love." His loving kindness is like the pity of a father for his children. It is forgiving, healing, redeeming, renewing. It is from everlasting to everlasting. It is on the throne which rules over all.

In vs. 6 (King James Version) another important word is given, "righteousness." This denotes God's act of setting things right, of establishing justice. God executes righteousness. That is his work. He shows it in establishing justice for the oppressed. God's righteousness is his loving kindness at work. Psalm 103 carries us directly to God, that we may know the One True God who gives unity to all that we find in the Old Testament. It is by standing in this redeeming grace that the various elements can be seen in proper perspective.

5

THE PROPHETS: PART 1, MOSES TO ELIJAH

THE PROPHETS—that is, the collection of the books of the prophets—is one of the main divisions of the Old Testament. "The Law and the Prophets" was a common way of speaking of the Old Testament. These Books of the Prophets not only constitute the largest division of the Old Testament but also are of special importance to Christian readers.

Our Christian education, both from the pulpit and in the classroom, has been weak at the point of making Christians acquainted with these key men, their work, and their writings. Our instruction generally has been limited to certain great passages, and our people have been left sadly ignorant of the work of God in the prophets. But they were the key men in God's work in the Old Testament. Nowhere in history before Christ came can so important a group of men be found.

The prophets were men especially called of God at point after point in history. They were the voice of God as he spoke to Israel. They interpreted the history of Israel— past, present, and future. "Thus says the Lord" was the constantly recurring word of these spokesmen of God. The Christian teacher should know five things regarding each of these men: (1) the name of the prophet, (2) the time and situation to which that prophet was called, (3) his

message from God to that situation, (4) the structure and
character of his book, (5) God's revelation of himself in
the prophet and his book. To be a good teacher of the
Old Testament, one should learn to give a brief sketch of
the life and work of each of the great prophets.

1. THE NAMES AND ORDER OF THE BOOKS OF THE PROPHETS

There are three ways of arranging these books. Each
arrangement is important. The order which we commonly
use is that which we find in the English Bible. Earlier, in
the Hebrew scriptures, a different order is found—the one
which was in use in New Testament times. Then there
is another valuable listing which seeks to place these books
in their historical sequence so that we may see each prophet
in his time in history. These three orders do not differ
a great deal, but each gives a helpful view for the thoughtful reader.

(a) The Order in the English Bible

ISAIAH	JEREMIAH	EZEKIEL	DANIEL

THE MAJOR PROPHETS
that is,
THE LARGER BOOKS

HOSEA	JOEL	AMOS	OBADIAH	JONAH	MICAH	NAHUM	HABAKKUK	ZEPHANIAH	HAGGAI	ZECHARIAH	MALACHI

THE MINOR PROPHETS
that is,
THE SMALLER BOOKS

Familiarity with the names of these books and the order
in which they are found in our English Bibles is a first
step in getting acquainted with these men of God. Turning in the Bible to each of these books, one after another,
learning the names of the prophets, observing the size of

each book, and refreshing the memory is a good preliminary exercise.

(b) The Order in the Hebrew Scriptures

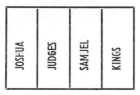

THE FORMER PROPHETS   THE LATTER PROPHETS

Compare this list as found in the Hebrew scriptures, with that in our English Bible. This was the order in use in Jesus' day and in the early church. The first group of four books, called the Former Prophets, we call books of history. They are books containing history, but in them the history was written as the proclamation of the word of God, that is, as words of prophecy. To the Hebrews, the prophets were not only speakers to the present but also were writers of history who told the story of the past to interpret God's will for the present. This is an important fact to keep in mind when we attempt to define the words "prophet" and "prophecy." The history of the past, written as we have it in the Former Prophets, is prophecy.

The Latter Prophets were listed as four, that is, they were in four scrolls. The fourth of these was called The Twelve. It included all those books which we call the Minor Prophets. In the English Bible we follow the same order in listing the names of these twelve small books. The Hebrews gathered them into one large scroll.

Another noticeable difference is in the placing of the Book of Daniel. In the Hebrew canon, Daniel is far down the list among what they called The Writings (see page 17). It was a late book among the Hebrew writings. It differs in many ways from the Books of Isaiah, Jeremiah, and Ezekiel. The Christian church promoted Daniel and placed his scroll with these three large scrolls of important prophets.

(c) **The Historical Order of the Prophets and Their Books.** In neither the Hebrew nor the Christian arrangement are the books placed consistently in their historical sequence. A good deal of illumination comes when we see these men one after another as God called them to situation after situation. This helps in seeing God at work step by step in the revelation of himself and his will. This order is not difficult to learn because in some instances certain books already stand in their correct time order.

The following table places the majority of the books in their historical order. (This basic table will help in considering others.)

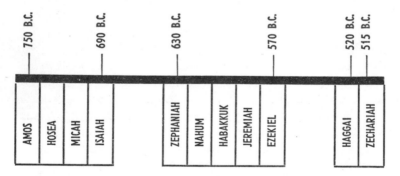

In this textbook three lessons are devoted to the prophets. This chapter considers the earliest group, Moses to Elijah. The next chapter deals with the eight-century prophets: Amos, Hosea, Isaiah, and Micah. The third lesson covers the group from Zephaniah to Zechariah; that is to say, the prophets of the end of the kingdom, the Exile, and the Restoration.

2. MOSES, THE FOUNTAINHEAD OF THE PROPHETS

Moses stands at the head of the prophets. He is the fountainhead of prophecy. One of the greatest panels of the prophets is that by Sargent in the Boston Public Library. In this impressive mural, showing the whole line of prophets, the artist places Moses at the center and magnifies him above all the others by means of elaborate artistic symbolism. Sargent is saying in the language of art that which the Book of Deuteronomy declares: "There has not arisen a prophet since in Israel like Moses" (Deut. 34:10).

We are so accustomed to speaking of Moses as the Lawgiver that we fail to give him his title of prophet. Moses was a prophet, a true spokesman of God, called by God to speak the word of God to Israel at a particular time. Recall the story of his call and commissioning and of his work as the spokesman of God at Mt. Sinai. God used Moses in speaking to Israel in their slavery. God used Moses as his mouthpiece at the Deliverance at the Red Sea. God used Moses as his spokesman in the making of the covenant. God spoke through Moses in commandments, exhortations, judgments, and promises. In the forty years in the wilderness God used Moses to instruct and discipline Israel. All this was the work of a prophet. We can see in the work of Moses what it meant to be a prophet. He defines the word for us.

But especially God called Moses to make his name known to Israel. It was through Moses that the name Yahweh became the name of God among his people. Every prophet thereafter declared, "Thus says Yahweh" or "It is the oracle of Yahweh." Review what was said on pp. 40-43 regarding the name. In the deliverance from Egypt and the covenant, Israel learned this unique name because they learned to know God in a unique way.

Moses taught Israel to worship Yahweh and him only because Yahweh is different from all the other gods. He is distinctive, peculiar, unique. "You shall have no other gods before me," for they are all different in character. For Israel there is one and only one God whom they should worship; His name is Yahweh. "You shall not make yourself a graven image, or any likeness of anything that is in heaven above, or that is in the earth beneath, or that is in the water under the earth; you shall not bow down to them or serve them; for I Yahweh your God am a jealous God."

The word "jealous" causes the reader some difficulty because we use it to denote a wrong human disposition. Not so here. Yahweh is different from all the gods—essentially and basically different. He is unique, the only one of his kind. The word "god" has a different meaning in Yahweh. He is for Israel the one and only one, the true and only God, the all-sufficient God. "You shall love Yahweh your God with all your heart, and with all your soul, and with all might" (Deut. 6:4). Moses' great work was to reveal this name of God and to bind Israel to worship Yahweh with such complete devotion that they would mention no other name. In this sense God is a jealous God, the one who is to be worshiped with all that is within his people.

The work of the prophets was a carrying on of the work of Moses. They were called to remind Israel that they must worship Yahweh and him only. Their work was to teach Israel in age after age about Yahweh and his will for Israel.

3. FROM MOSES TO ELIJAH

After Moses the next top name among the prophets was Elijah. Between these two giants there are a number of less prominent names, but each had an appointed work. They were all oral prophets who left no writings. It was sufficient for each of them to speak to his generation. There are many references to little known prophets, even to some nameless messengers. The period from Moses to Elijah covered a long stretch of time. It included the entering into the Promised Land, the consolidation of the tribes into a kingdom, and the earlier history of the kingdom. These times were full of problems in keeping Israel true to the worship of Yahweh. "You shall have no other gods before me" was a difficult commandment in the midst of tribal rivalries, wars with threatening foes, political ambitions, and the constant allurements of the worship of the baals. A brief time line will show this period in the large. (See the fuller time line for details.)

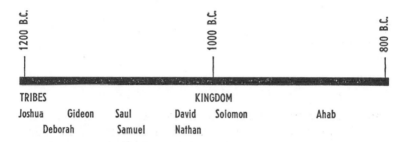

many references to little known prophets, even to some

1200 B.C.			1000 B.C.			800 B.C.
TRIBES			KINGDOM			
Joshua	Gideon	Saul	David	Solomon		Ahab
	Deborah	Samuel	Nathan			

(a) Deborah, the Revivalist (Judges, chaps. 4-5). This prophetess appeared on the scene briefly at a time of crisis. It was when Israel was very seriously threatened and was in danger of losing that devotion to Yahweh which Moses had awakened in them. The Hebrews were living as tribes scattered throughout Palestine with no organized government. Each tribe was centered in its own life. Each tribe was indifferent toward or was an enemy of the other tribes.

In one of these crises, Deborah arose and rallied enough neighboring tribes to meet the immediate local danger (Judg. 4:4-10). Deborah was a revivalist, a Yahweh en-

thusiast who stirred up enough tribes to resist the threat of
destruction. Reading the fiery spirit of this woman in her
poem, Judges 5, we can understand what a prophet was in
that day. Deborah was the voice of God for Israel at that
particular time, rallying the tribes to go to battle against
their foe. In Deborah one can see that a prophet was a revivalist, an arouser, a herald.

(b) **Samuel, the King-Maker** (1 Sam. 1:1—25:1).
This prophet arose at a time when the life of the Hebrews
was again at a low ebb. The Philistines were pushing into
the country and making the people of Israel their slaves.
The Hebrews were divided and fearful. They had to be
brought together as one nation, under one leader who could
awaken courage and make them strong enough to win the
battle against the Philistines. Samuel was raised up for such
a time. First, he inspired Saul to become the leader of Israel.
After Saul's failure, he chose David and anointed him. So
Samuel did his work as a prophet in calling and guiding
the king when Israel was threatened with weakness and in-
vasion. But his chief work was to recall his people to true
Yahweh worship, to serve Yahweh and him only, to trust
in Yahweh as their only deliverer. The king must hearken
to the voice of the prophet, for the prophet is God's spokesman. Samuel's message is clearly stated in 1 Samuel 12:24:
"Only fear the Lord [Yahweh], and serve him faithfully
with all your heart; for consider what great things he has
done for you."

(c) **Nathan** (2 Sam. 11:1—12:14). This prophet
appeared after David had established his kingdom and had
come into real kingly power. David was an enthusiastic
worshiper of Yahweh, a very active and devoted follower
of the God of Israel. But David, as king, was stirred by
strong ambition for power and glory. He was always in the
midst of temptation to use his position and authority for

his own ends. Like any king, David was likely to say "*My* kingdom come, *my* will be done." This spirit of tyranny appears in the story of Bathsheba and Uriah. To take another man's wife and to have her husband killed seemed permissible to a king. But at this point Nathan the Prophet appeared before the king to declare the king's guilt. Nathan was God's spokesman. He was commissioned to declare to the king God's word of judgment and condemnation, but also God's word of forgiveness when the king repented.

These three are representative prophets in the period from Moses to Elijah: Deborah, who rallied the tribes to unite in the name of Yahweh; Samuel, who in the name of Yahweh formed the tribes into a kingdom; and Nathan, who in the name of Yahweh condemned the king for injustice. Compare the idea of a king in 1 Samuel 8:11-17 with that in Psalm 72. The first passage states the practice of the tyrant; the second states the ideal of the prophets.

4. ELIJAH (1 KINGS 17:1—19:21; 21:1-29; 2 KINGS 1:1—2:18).

This fiery soul has spoken to the imagination and the conscience of mankind with peculiar power. He was sent to his people at a time of crisis when the internal conflict between contradictory forces demanded a man of exceptional vigor. On the one side of this contest was justice; on the other side was kingly power. On the one side was the simple Hebrew village life with its strong sense of freedom and equality; on the other side was royal ostentation and the denial of the rights of the people. On the one side was the rugged peasant Elijah, fired with wholehearted devotion to Yahweh; on the other side was the proud queen Jezebel, burning with devotion for Baal Melkart, the god of Tyre.

This conflict, therefore, was the collision of two contradictory ideas of God and man. Jezebel was a worshiper of Baal Melkart, a god of military might and kingly tyranny. Elijah was a worshiper of the God of loving-kindness and justice who had delivered Israel from bondage to a tyrant. Jezebel was the daughter of a usurper who by arms had made himself master of the rich, prosperous lands of Tyre and Sodom. Elijah was a common man, one of the poor of the land, whose precious possession was equality and freedom. Between these two dominant characters of the drama stood Ahab, the king of Israel. He knew the God of justice, but he had the ambition of a king in power. The word of Elijah touched his conscience: the word of Jezebel, his wife touched his ambition. Ahab limped between the two. He was a worshiper of Yahweh, but he would also include Baal. And the nation was limping between the two. Elijah's challenge goes to the heart of this conflict in which there can be no compromise. "How long will you go limping with two different opinions? If the Lord [Yahweh] is God, follow him; but if Baal, then follow him" (1 Kings 18:21).

The story of this intense conflict is one of the best told stories in the Old Testament. It needs to be read through to feel its power. As noted above, this conflict was the collision of two concepts of God and man. To understand this, the meaning of the word "baal" must be considered. Baal means owner. Baal is the equivalent of master. It was used as the title of the owner of property or of a wife. Baal denoted a position of power over people or things. When applied to a god it indicated power without moral character. The idea of God learned under Moses in the Deliverance and Covenant was the very opposite of this.

The ancient people of Palestine fancied that all nature was owned and controlled by baalim; i.e., by masters. Each tree, spring, mountain, field, had its baal. The baalim, they thought, gave the fertility of the flocks, the herds, the family. So they must worship each baal according to its requirements. When the Hebrews settled as farmers in Canaan they were in the midst of this worship. The secret of fertility, according to the old inhabitants of the land, was in certain fertility rites full of the magic which, it was believed, would gain the favor of the baalim. The people of Yahweh were attracted to this kind of worship. Some Hebrews turned to the baalim and forsook their own God. Some compromised and worshiped both. Others used the title "baal" with the name of their god.

In the worship of these nature gods, there was much magical ceremony and many incantations. Read, in 1 Kings 18:26-29, the account of the ritualistic dancing and self-mutilation of the priests of baal, with their repeated incantations. In the harvest festivals, especially the grape harvest, the worship of the baalim became wild, debauched, and sensual. Baalism was a corrupting and debasing influence. "Choose," was Elijah's strong imperative.

The story of Naboth demonstrates the issue of justice. Read 1 Kings 21:1-16. Naboth was a small landowner in the town of Jezreel, a Hebrew freeman among Hebrew freemen. Before their God the people of Israel were equal and justice was the law of their community life. No one had authority over another. Naboth held his property as a heritage; that is, as a stewardship handed on from generation to generation and therefore not an item of trade. Further, it was only as a landowner that he stood as a freeman in his village. There was no class of hired laborers. Loss of property would mean serfdom. Now enters King Ahab, wanting to enlarge the grounds of his country dwelling in Jezreel. Naboth stands on his rights against the demands and bribes of the king. Freedom and justice are the creed of this worshiper of God of justice and faithfulness. Jezebel, the wife of Ahab, is a baal worshiper. She intervenes with no sense of justice or of the rights of the common man. To her way of thinking, a king has the right of a master which a citizen opposes at the price of his life. Any means of power can be used by the king. Into this scene of the brutal violation of the right, the prophet Elijah suddenly appears. This blazing champion of the God of justice stands before Ahab in the very piece of land secured by the blood of an innocent man and his family. There he speaks the word of God. This is what being a prophet means. The story should be read over and over, with close attention and imaginative insight, until it becomes deeply lodged in the soul as the prophetic word.

The story of the contest on Mt. Carmel shows this conflict in another aspect. Read 1 Kings 18:1-46. Who is the God who gives rain and fertility to the land? The account of this day-long contest is one of the most dramatic in the Old Testament. The giving of fertility was attributed to the baalim. Elijah challenged the baal worshipers at the point of their greatest claim. The priests of baal practiced their ritual of magic, but all in vain. Elijah's faith in the God of Israel was constant through the day. Finally he made his sacrifice, offered his simple prayer, and then looked to the west from which the clouds come which break the dry season—and the rains came! What the people needed at that time was a demonstration. In this contest they had it in this striking event to which they could appeal. It helped their faith.

The story of Elijah at Horeb shows the contest in another phase. See 1 Kings 19:1-21. The contest on Mt. Carmel had exhausted Elijah. Following the intense excitement, Elijah was in low spirits, and the threat of the powerful and determined Jezebel frightened him. He fled to faraway Horeb (Sinai), where God had made his initial revelation and had established his covenant. Elijah needed renewal and fresh consecration. In the mountain storm (the wind, the earthquake, and the fire) which demonstrated only power, Elijah did not find the answer to his need. Then came the Voice. The contrast is between a Noise and a Voice, between the outward demonstration of power and the communication of person with person. The famous expression, "And after the fire a still small voice," does not give the true force of this statement. Read the statement thus: "And after the fire a Voice, a Voice muted to a whisper." The emphasis should be upon "Voice." God speaks, communicates, makes his will known. So Elijah was given a new commission and returned to his work.

The account of Elijah's translation climaxes the story. See 2 Kings 2:1-18. What a dramatic, fiery ending for this dramatic prophet of justice and of single-hearted devotion to the God of righteousness.

5. THE MEANING OF THE WORDS "PROPHESY" AND "PROPHECY"

Looking back over the prophets from Moses to Elijah, what meanings are evident for these words? What did a prophet do? What was his work? The student must carefully examine the accounts of the prophets as given in the Old Testament to see just what a prophet was and did. The essential fact is this: A prophet was a spokesman of God, sent to speak to Israel in certain situations. The introduction to these words is, "Thus says Yahweh." They were men who were moved by the spirit of God and told the nation what they had heard and seen.

In our everyday language the words "prophet," "prophecy," and "prophesy" are used constantly with the meanings of current thinking. An English dictionary gives a definition according to present usage. According to current usage a prophet is a *foreteller,* a *predictor.* We speak of a weather prophet, indicating one who tells about future weather. So, in common practice, "prophesying" refers to predicting and "prophecy" is a foretelling of the future. There is a tendency to impose upon the Old Testament words this modern meaning. But we must go back to the prophets of the Old Testament and see in them what was meant by this word. The word "prophet" is one which the English language has taken over from the Greek. The Hebrews had their own word, which is not at all like our English word. NABI was their word. It does not say anything about prediction. NABI was used by men upon whom the spirit of God came. They said what they said and did what they did because the spirit of God was at work in them.

When the Hebrew scriptures were translated into Greek, the Greek word PROPHETES (singular number) was used. This Greek word was used for one who stood in front of a shrine and declared the word of the god. "Pro" means "in front of." The Greek *prophetes* was a spokesman, a declarer, an interpreter. Although a *prophetes* might predict, the Greek word in itself does not mean a "predictor." Nor does the Hebrew word.

When we read of the Hebrew prophets, we discover that their primary task was to speak to their present, to their immediate situation. As a spokesman of God the prophet dealt with the affairs of his day. See how true this was of Moses, Deborah, Samuel, Nathan, and Elijah. But no present stands by itself. Each present is bound both to the past and to the future. Old Testament prophets spoke of the past, the present, and the future. They recalled the past, interpreted the present, forecast the future; for all times belong together in God's purpose for his chosen people. So each prophet brought to the times to which he was called the insight needed to understand God in that day, the same yesterday, today, and forever.

6

THE PROPHETS: PART 2, THE ASSYRIAN CRISIS

THE FOUR PROPHETS, Amos, Hosea, Isaiah, and Micah, belong together as God's spokesmen in the period of the Assyrian crisis; that is to say, from about 750 B.C. to 690 B.C. These four men, each in his own way, spoke to the same national and world situation. Assyria was pushing westward in campaign after campaign. Kingdom after kingdom fell before those competent, ruthless conquerors. The Northern Kingdom was utterly destroyed. The Southern Kingdom was made a vassal state. These prophets labored to bring to Israel the moral insight needed to meet this advance of Assyria. They called upon Israel to see the sin of the nation, their departure from their God. They besought the nation to return to God.

These four men were as one in their divine inspiration. Although they differed in their native gifts and in their local situations, all spoke the same fundamental message: "Behold, the eyes of the Lord Jehovah are upon the sinful kingdom, and I will destroy it from off the face of the earth" (Amos 9:8, ASV). These four men were prophets of doom for each and every sinful kingdom. But also they were prophets who pointed the way in which God can cause a nation to live. In the Assyrian crisis these men were prophets both of judgment and of promise. Amos, the keen-thinking shepherd of Tekoa; Hosea, the anguished husband in the baal-corrupted village; Micah, the voice of the dispossessed farmers; Isaiah, the lofty-minded aristocrat of Jerusalem—how diverse in gifts, yet how at one in inspiration!

1. The Assyrian Crisis. These four messengers are called the eighth-century prophets, because they were sent to Israel in the last half of the eighth century B.C., 740-690 (Note that the seven hundreds are the eighth century.) That century was critical in ancient history because in it Assyria fought its way to world dominion and changed the affairs of all the peoples of that day. There were constant wars and rumors of war. There was conquest after conquest in which lands were devastated in merciless warfare. Those who could seize power used it for the exploitation of their victims. By military might kings and rulers established themselves with no regard to the rights of others. The eighth century B.C. was a period of widespread, destructive injustice.

The tension in Palestine was between Assyria, the aggressive, swift campaigner with the new equipments of militarism (see Isa. 10:5-14) and Egypt, the sluggish, futile schemer (see Isa. 19:1-17). The kings of Palestine were either pro-Assyrian or pro-Egyptian as they played their foolish game of politics. "Ephraim [the Northern Kingdom] is like a dove, silly and without sense, calling to Egypt, going to Assyria" (Hos. 7:11). But Assyria kept moving westward, advancing toward world dominion—a fact hard for Israel to see and harder to accept. Four great military tyrants, in wave after wave of conquest, swept over Palestine with destructive military might. Finally in 722 B.C. Assyria destroyed the Northern Kingdom utterly and reduced the Southern Kingdom to a weak vassal. Tiglathpileser (745-727), Shalmaneser (727-722), Sargon (722-705), and Sennacherib (705-681) reduced all other powers, large and

small, until Assyria stood triumphant in the sinful pride
of its great city, Nineveh. The Assyrians were proud, ruthless
boastful, destructive militarists who smashed their way across
the world and bragged about it in their propaganda
bulletins.

As one reads Amos, Hosea, Isaiah, and Micah, he should
hear the march of armies, listen to the plots and counter-
plots of men ambitious for power, hear the cries of the
suffering, discern the rot of injustice which was destroying
both the Northern and the Southern Kingdoms at a time
when they needed their full strength to survive. "Therefore
I am like a moth to Ephraim, and like dry rot to the house
of Judah. When Ephraim saw his sickness, and Judah his
wound, then Ephraim went to Assyria, and sent to the great
king [a contemptuous term for Egypt]. But he is not able
to cure you, or heal your wound" (Hos. 5:12-13). God
called these men to speak directly to the Hebrews of the
eighth-century situation. Their word becomes clear when
that century is known in some measure.

2. Amos. The Book of Amos stands in third place in
that collection of small books of prophecy known in the
Hebrew canon as the Book of the Twelve and in the Christian canon as the Minor Prophets. It is a very small book,
what we today would call a pamphlet. Because of its small-
ness, its place in a collection of small books, and the absence
of any reference to Amos in other books of the Bible, Amos
does not often receive the attention he deserves. In historical
order the Book of Amos stands first in the list. His is the
earliest written prophecy. When Amos is understood, he
is recognized as one of the greatest of the Old Testament
prophets.

We have no story of Amos. All we know about him
we gain from a careful reading of his book in the light of
what history tells us about his times. In this way we can

become well acquainted with him. Amos was among the shepherds of Tekoa in the days of Uzziah, king of Judah, and of Jeroboam II, king of Israel (Amos 1:1). He calls himself a herdsman and a dresser of sycamore trees (Amos 7:14) and asserts that God called him from following the flock to preach against the house of Isaac. So we know him to have been a humble shepherd.

Tekoa, about ten miles south of Jerusalem, was in the barren wastes of Judah, a land of droughts and wild animals. The task of a shepherd in the wilderness required alertness, endurance, bravery, pity, and patience, all the qualities of the good shepherd of the Twenty-third Psalm. The wool from the flocks had to be taken to the central markets of the land, where people gathered from far and near for the great festivals. At these sanctuary-markets Amos could learn what was going on in his own country under the kingship of Uzziah and also in the Northern Kingdom under the rule of Jeroboam II. Also he could get from the traders the news about the nearby nations: Damascus (1:3), Gaza (1:6), Tyre (1:9), Edom (1:11), Ammon (1:13), and Moab (2:1). And from beyond these small kingdoms came news regarding the great empires of Egypt and Assyria.

Amos was sent to the Northern Kingdom, Israel, whose king, Jeroboam II, was the particular object of his condemnation. Note, "In the days of Jeroboam" (1:1). "I will rise against the house [the dynasty] of Jeroboam with the sword" (7:10). This Jeroboam reigned from 785 to 744 B.C. He was the strongest, most successful ruler in the history of the Northern Kingdom. With Uzziah he attained a glory equal to that of Solomon (2 Kings 14:25).

The Book of Amos is a series of condemnations of the rule of Jeroboam for tyranny, oppression, corruption, greed, lust, and injustice. See 2:6-8; 3:10; 4:1; 5:10-12. About the year 750 B.C., Amos made these declarations time and again. The kingdom was completely destroyed in 722 B.C. The sinful kingdom and the sinful political order of power and greed came to its certain doom in the moral rule of God. In Amos God makes his demand for justice. "Hate evil, and love good, and establish justice in the gate" (5:15). "Let justice roll down like waters, and righteousness like an overflowing stream" (5:24). In Amos God stood in the midst of Israel as a man with a plumb line demanding the nation should be erect in righteousness or it would fall as a leaning wall (7:7-9).

In 1:3—2:16 Amos opens his preaching against the house of Israel. He stood at the entrance of the royal sanctuary of King Jeroboam in Bethel where he could speak to all the people of Israel, especially to the rulers. His method is interesting. First he brings God's moral judgment against their neighbors, foes or friends of Israel, for their acts of injustice and then against Israel for its act of injustice. For one and all there is one moral law. Therefore there is one moral judgment and one doom. Each and every sinful kingdom is to be destroyed. Amos is seeking to awaken the conscience of Israel.

The judgment against Israel is stronger than that against the other peoples, for they are the chosen people who have been instructed in the law of their God. God gave Amos exceptional insight when he gave his prophet these words to the people whom he brought out of Egypt (note the great event of God's mercy and justice): "You only have I known of all the families [the whole earth]: *therefore* I will punish you for all your iniquities" (3:2). Election does not mean privilege but deeper responsibility, allegiance, covenant, and therefore judgment. Amos makes this the more emphatic when he gives this searching word of the God of justice: "Are you not like the Ethiopians to me, O people of Israel?" says Yahweh. "Did I not bring up Israel

from the land of Egypt, and the Philistines from Caphtor
and the Syrians from Kir?" (9:7). There is one moral Ruler,
one moral Law, one divine Purpose. Worship must be
moral, not a means of escaping consequences. (See 2:8;
4:4-5; 5:21-24.) In Amos God gives his basic word in
prophecy. All other prophets declare the same fundamental
truth. The prophets are God's messengers demanding
justice. The key words of Amos are, "Hate evil, and love
good, and establish justice in the gate" (5:15), and "Let
justice roll down like waters, and righteousness like an ever-
flowing stream" (5:24).

3. Hosea. The Book of Hosea stands in first place in
that collection of small books of prophecy known in the
Hebrew canon as the Book of the Twelve and in the Christian canon as the Minor Prophets. Again we deal with a small
book which we would call a pamphlet. In historical order
the Book of Hosea stands second in the list, just a few years
after Amos.

We have no story of Hosea. Once again, all we know
about him we gain from careful reading of his book in the
light of what history tells us about his times. Hosea was
a self-revealing man into whose heart one can enter under-
standingly. He was different from Amos, as tenderness is
different from sternness, but both were moved by the same
pity for their people, the same insistent demand for the
righteousness of God. Amos demanded justice: Hosea demanded fealty. Both were making essentially the same
demand.

Hosea came from a village in the fertile, rich country of
the north. He belonged to one of the chief families and
married the daughter of another leading house. "Hosea the
son of Beeri" (1:1); "Gomer the daughter of Diblaim"
(1:3). The story of these two is a tragedy, for their mar-
riage was ruined by the sensuality of the fertility celebration

taken over from the native baal worship. The harvest festivals easily degenerated into licentious practices. Gomer was enticed into these orgies, entered into harlotry, and consequently landed in slavery. Hosea's love for his wife was constant: he kept his troth. Finally he bought Gomer out of her slavery that he might heal her of her unfaithfulness. Just how it all ended is not told. Therefore the interpreter must be careful not to oversentimentalize the story and give it a modern romantic ending which is not found in this book. Suffice it to say that the love of Hosea revealed that redeeming grace which seeks to cause the faithless to return and be healed.

Hosea knew the redeeming love of Yahweh for his faithless people, Israel. God's love taught Hosea to love Gomer and his experience of loving Gomer taught him God's love for Israel. The story begins with Yahweh's love. "When Israel was a child, I loved him, and out of Egypt I called my son" (11:1). The message of Hosea to faithless Israel is "Return." "Return, O Israel, to the Lord [Yahweh] your God, for you have stumbled because of your iniquity. Take with you words and return to the Lord" (14:1).

But, declares Hosea, the Lord has cause for the condemnation and destruction of his sinful people, Israel. "The Lord has a controversy with the inhabitants of the land. There is no faithfulness or kindness, and no knowledge of God in the land; there is swearing, lying, killing, stealing, and committing adultery; they break all bounds and murder follows murder" (4:1-2). See 4:14-16; 5:14; 8:11-14; 10:1-2, 13-15; 13:7-8, 16. Because of this, Israel will be destroyed. Hosea predicts doom just as certainly as does Amos. (See 13:4-16.) The sinful kingdom brings destruction upon itself. But in this awareness of the end at hand there is the strong feeling of redeeming love. Hosea 11:1—12:1 is one of the most profound passages in the Scriptures.

In it we see the agony of love, the mind tossed to and fro between the sad fact of Israel's refusal to return to God and God's desire to bring his people to faithfulness. Hosea, possessed by the mind of God, plumbed the depths of this tragedy of love.

Thus, in Hosea, God reaches more deeply into his basic word in prophecy. In Hosea that great word HESED, loving-kindness, faithful covenant love, is emphasized. The God of Israel is the God whose pledged love endures forever. He is ever seeking this same fealty in his people.

4. **Micah.** The Book of Micah stands sixth among the prophets called the Minor Prophets. All that is recorded of him is, "The Word of the Lord that came to Micah of Moresheth in the days of Jotham, Ahaz, and Hezekiah, kings of Judah, which he saw concerning Samaria and Jerusalem" (1:1). The town of Moresheth was in the western lowlands near the city of Gath, a land of small farms open to the coming and going of the armies. For this reason, it was in economic distress; the farmers became debt-ridden. Their holdings became mortgaged and fell into the hands of absentee lords in Samaria and Jerusalem. Micah was the voice of these oppressed farmers who were passing into serfdom. "Woe to those who devise wickedness and work evil upon their beds! When the morning dawns, they perform it, because it is in the power of their hand. They covet fields and seize them; and houses, and take them away; they oppress a man and his house, a man and his inheritance" (2:1-2). "Hear, you heads of Jacob and rulers of the house of Israel! Is it not for you to know justice?—you who hate the good and love the evil, who tear the skin from off my people, and their flesh from off their bones; who eat the flesh of my people, and flay their skin from off them, and break their bones in pieces, and chop them up like meat in a kettle, like flesh in a caldron" (3:1-3).

Micah is best known for his penetrating statement of true religion: "To do justice, and to love kindness, and to walk humbly with your God" (6:8). So this man of the common people, the oppressed common people who were denied justice and kindness, spoke the everlasting mind of God. In Micah 4:1-4 the message of peace is given. This is found also in Isaiah 2:1-4 and will be considered in the study of Isaiah.

5. Isaiah. The book of the prophecies of Isaiah stands first in every collection of the prophets. It has priority not only because it is one of the earliest of the written prophecies, but also because of its fullness and evangelical power. In historical order it stands in third place along with Micah, the contemporary of Isaiah.

The ministry of Isaiah lasted from about 740 B.C., to 690 B.C., the longest period of continuous prophetic ministry of any of the prophets. In that half-century of Assyrian advance, Isaiah was called to speak to kings and people in the name of the Holy One who is the King of kings and Lord of lords. So we know a good deal of his story. Isaiah was of the city of Jerusalem, evidently a member of the aristocracy—that aristocacy which he condemned for injustice and oppression.

Isaiah's life falls into three main divisions: (1) From 740 B.C. to 734 B.C., the early public ministry, from his opening vision (chap. 6) to the time when Ahaz became the vassal of Pul or Tiglathpileser, the Assyrian conqueror. During this period, the young prophet did all he could to lead the young king, Ahaz, to put his faith in God (Yahweh), but the king chose the foolish way of buying the protection of Tiglathpileser at the cost of a vassalage in which Ahaz acknowledged the power of Ashur, the god of Assyria. (2) From 734 B.C. to 713 B.C., the middle period. For about twenty-one years Isaiah withdrew from exhorting the king and devoted himself to training disciples. He saw the need for a religious minority, instructed as the core of the nation, a pious remnant. (3) In 713 he appeared again. This time as God's messenger to King Hezekiah in another crisis when the Assyrians under Sennacherib were threatening the very life of Jerusalem. Tradition says that Isaiah died the martyr's death under the evil persecutor, Manasseh, King of Judah.

During the long period of Isaiah's ministry there was the constant advance of Assyria in war after war of conquest. This was the prime concern of all the people, of kings, lords, merchants, farmers, slaves. What to do regarding Assyria? There was no peace in the eighth century. Instead there was the constant fighting of pro-Assyrian parties and anti-Assyrian advocates. Pro-Assyrian aspirants for power murdered anti-Assyrians and then anti-Assyrians murdered pro-Assyrians. Read 2 Kings 15:1—21:9. Coalition after coalition arose to withstand Assyria, but none was able to meet this mighty power and none held together, because all of them were made up of ambitious rivals. Accordingly, God's word to Isaiah was: "Do not call conspiracy all that this people call conspiracy, and do not fear what they fear, nor be in dread. But the Lord of hosts, him you shall regard as holy; let him be your fear, and let him be your dread" (8:12-13).

The key verse for understanding Isaiah in the face of the world crisis is 30:15: "For thus said the Lord God, the Holy One of Israel, 'In returning and rest you shall be saved; in quietness and trust shall be your strength.'" But kings and lords refused to hearken. Foolishly they attempted to match their military weakness against the mighty armies from Nineveh. "And you would not [return to God and rest in him], but you said 'No! We will speed upon horses, . . . We will ride upon swift steeds.'" (30:16). Isaiah is

called the prophet of faith. His was a very robust coura-
geous faith when confronted by triumphant, overwhelming military might. From his young manhood to his old
age and martyrdom, Isaiah found his strength in the Holy
One of Israel and in quietness in the midst of constant fears
and dreads.

It all began with the vision of God, the Holy One seated
upon the throne. Chapter 6 is one of the key chapters in
the whole Old Testament. Isaiah, the young aristocrat, was
worshiping in the Temple. Suddenly there came one of
those moments of inspiration which change lives completely.
He saw the God of Israel as he had never seen him before.
The word "holy" is an all-important term. Gods were always called holy, but this might mean only powerful magic.
But when Isaiah heard the heavenly beings singing "Holy!
Holy!! Holy!!! is Yahweh of hosts; the whole earth is full
of his glory," holiness took on a different meaning. This
song produced the sense of sin. "Woe is me! For I am
lost; for I am a man of unclean lips, and I dwell in the midst
of a people of unclean lips; for my eyes have seen the King,
the Lord [Yahweh] of hosts!" Holiness now means perfect
moral character. "The Lord of hosts is exalted in justice,
and the Holy God shows himself holy in righteousness"
(5:16). "Holy" means righteousness among people. "For
the Lord is a God of justice" (30:18). The commandment
of the Holy One to his people is, "Wash yourselves; make
yourselves clean; remove the evil of your doings from be-
for my eyes; cease to do evil, learn to do good; seek justice,
correct oppression; defend the fatherless, plead for the
widow" (1:16-17). The angelic song, "Holy! Holy!!
Holy!!!" made Isaiah the passionate pleader for justice.

Isaiah saw the Lord upon a throne high and lifted up.
Others saw earthly kings on their thrones: kings of Israel
and Judah, kings of Egypt and Assyria. Isaiah saw that

the one and only king of heaven and earth is the Holy
One. So Isaiah had no fear of any earthly ruler. The only
one to fear or dread is the one upon the throne over all the
world. In this faith Isaiah found and proclaimed quietness
and trust. He condemned Israel in the most severe terms, but
Isaiah is the prophet of great hopes, of a glorious future.
Two of the passages treasured by the church celebrate the
inspired faith and hope of Isaiah, namely, 9:2-7 and 11:1-9.
An ideal ruler, an ideal kingdom, and the earth full of the
knowledge of the Lord! That vision came in the face of
the most ruthless military tyranny in all history. Such is
the miracle of prophecy.

6. **The Eighth-Century Prophets as a Whole.** These
four men together form one of God's effective teams for
the revelation of his name and the instruction of his people.
Their words are words of spirit and truth. They are understood in the time and circumstances of their proclamation.
On the one side was the conceit of power of the Hebrew
kings, military lords, merchant lords: on the other side
were the smashing conquerors from Assyria. Against both
of these tyrannies were these four voices without any outward power or prestige. We can read today the proud
boastings of the Assyrian war lords in their own records
unearthed in the city of Nineveh. In their conceit of power
they bragged about their destructive campaigns in which
they burned city after city and left them in desolation. All
of them made bragging records of their deeds. They sent
their proclamations far and wide in conceited publicity. But
what was the end of these tyrants?

Isaiah scorned them and declared that God would destroy
them. And God did. Their cities were destroyed and their
royal records were buried in the ruins so that the only
knowledge of Tiglathpileser, Shalmaneser, Sargon, and
Sennacherib was that which was derived from the brief Old

Testament records. Today, however, their cities have been unearthed and their writings have been deciphered by biblical scholars. We know their story in detail. But this knowledge is useful to us chiefly in understanding these prophets. What a divine reversal of history! The kings who seemed to be the somebodies have become the nobodies, and the prophets who were despised and rejected have become the persons of lasting significance. Observe the reasons for the continuing importance of these messengers of the one moral rule.

(a) These prophets are of lasting significance because they stated the true meaning of religion and the true hope of the reign of God. Note their statements about what God requires of his people. The people of Israel made much of offering sacrifices, but they thought of sacrifices as a bribe to secure the favor of God. They supposed that a man might rob the poor and then use a part of the stolen property to make an offering which would appease God for the wrong done. Their worship became sin. "Come to Bethel, and transgress; to Gilgal, and multiply transgression; bring your sacrifices every morning [rather than three times a year], your tithes every three days [rather than yearly]; offer a sacrifice of thanksgiving of that which is leavened [going beyond the requirement], and proclaim freewill offerings, publish them [prideful publicity]; for so you love to do, O people of Israel" (Amos 4:4-5). Compare this with the searching condemnation of the worship in the Temple in Jerusalem (Isa. 1:10-15). Against this false worship of God the prophets state the nature of true devotion to the Holy One, the God of justice and righteousness.

"Let justice roll down like waters,
and righteousness like an ever-flowing stream" (Amos 5:24).

"For I desire steadfast love and not sacrifice,
The knowledge of God, rather than burnt offerings"
(Hos. 6:6).

"Wash yourselves; make yourselves clean;
    remove the evil of your doings
    from before my eyes;
  cease to do evil, learn to do good;
  seek justice, correct oppression;
  defend the fatherless, plead for the widow" (Isa. 1:16-17).

" 'With what shall I come before the Lord,
    and bow myself before God on high?
  Shall I come before him with burnt offerings,
    with calves a year old?
  Will the Lord be pleased with thousands of rams,
    with ten thousands of rivers of oil?
  Shall I give my first-born for my transgression,
    the fruit of my body for the sin of my soul?'
  He has showed you, O man, what is good;
    and what does the Lord require of you
  but to do justice, and to love kindness,
    and to walk humbly with your God?" (Micah 6:6-8).

(b) These prophets are of lasting significance because they pronounced God's moral judgment against sin. All four are prophets of DOOM. They promise the doom which is at hand for the sinful kingdom. "Behold, the eyes of the Lord Jehovah are upon the sinful kingdom, and I will destroy it from off the face of the earth" (Amos 9:8, ASV). The kingdoms of Israel and Judah were ruled by evil-minded militarists. So were the kingdoms of all the surrounding peoples—Damascus, Gaza, Edom, Moab, Ammon, Tyre (Amos 1:3—2:5). So were the empires of Assyria and Egypt. The prophets tell what will happen to such sinful governments. Sure to follow were all the disasters, cruelties, murderings that go with such kingdoms fighting one another for power. In 5:16-17 Amos pictures the desolation of invading armies. Compare Isaiah 1:7-9.

And this doom of the sinful kingdom came. The Northern Kingdom was utterly destroyed in 722 B.C. Sennacherib, in 701 B.C. shut Hezekiah up in Jerusalem like a bird in a cage, devastated all his territory, and left Judah like "a booth in a vineyard" (i.e., an old, abandoned, dilapidated shelter). Read again Isaiah 1:7-8.

(c) These prophets are of lasting significance because of their message of HOPE. They declare God's purpose regarding his people. The kingdoms might go down in deserved doom, but God still had a people. " 'Behold, the eyes of the Lord God are upon the sinful kingdom, and I will destroy it from the surface of the ground; except that I will not utterly destroy the house of Jacob,' says the Lord" (Amos 9:8). There is hope because God has a purpose for the house of Jacob, the chosen people. While the rulers and the majority of the people rebel and bring destruction, there will be a minority, a remnant, who will return to the Lord.

These words "remnant" and "return to the Lord" are important. Amos says, "Seek good, and not evil, that you may live; and so the Lord, the God of hosts, will be with you, as you have said. Hate evil, and love good, and establish justice in the gate; it may be that the Lord, the God of Hosts will be gracious to the remnant of Joseph [the Northern Kingdom]" (5:14-15). Amos does not express much hope, but hope there is. Hosea calls to his people to return. "Return, O Israel, to the Lord your God, for you have stumbled because of your iniquity. Take with you words and return to the Lord" (14:1-2). But Hosea was agonized for he saw only a superficial returning.

This returning could not be by easily spoken words. It would not do to say in superficial presumption, "Come, let us return to the Lord, for he has torn and he will heal" (Hos. 6:1). When Israel comes in this way, Hosea re-

plies: "Your love is like a morning cloud, like the dew
that goes early away" (6:4). No, something more drastic
was needed. They needed to be hewn by the prophets and
slain by the word of God (6:8). "I will turn my hand
against you and will smelt away your dross as with lye
and remove all your alloy. And I will restore your judges
as at the first, and your counselors as at the beginning.
Afterward you shall be called the city of righteousness, the
faithful city. Zion shall be redeemed by justice, and those
in her who repent, by righteousness" (Isa. 1:25-27). God
must make a new people in whom is the knowledge of
God. They must be washed, smelted by fire, redeemed.
They must repent and seek the good. God's act in the redemptive purging of the remnant who repent and return
is the hope of those eighth-century prophets.

For the restored city of righteousness, the faithful city,
there must be the true ruler. Evil kings and lords had been
the core of the sinful kingdom. It is Isaiah who in the
midst of the proud rulers of that day saw the true Ruler.
Two of his greatest passages which we treasure so deeply
in the church proclaim the leader whom God will give
to the nation. Read Isaiah 9:2-7 and 11:1-5. At a time
when the world had an utterly different idea, Isaiah hailed
the ideal Ruler. These passages state exactly the need of
the world at that time and for all time. We shall come
to these passages in relation to Jesus in the final chapter.

(d) These prophets are of lasting significance because
the true ideal of peace arose among them. Read again the
passage which appears in both Isaiah 2:14 and Micah
4:1-4. Consider the times in which this profound hope
appeared. There were no signs of peace. It was a war-
ridden world in which plowshares were beaten into swords
and pruning hooks into spears. Armies, conquests, nation
against nation—such was the order of the day. The prophets'

words in their day seemed utter nonsense. But recall what Isaiah did in the middle period of his ministry (see p. 79 ff.). Turning away from the vain effort to change the military mind of the king, he devoted himself to training disciples. He called about himself those who, repenting, returned to the Lord. He trained them in the knowledge of the Lord. In them there was a remnant who believed that the God of justice would establish justice. The hope of peace is rooted in this inspired act of Isaiah.

7. What, then, is a prophet? Look at these four men and from them gain your answer. What did these men do? Describe the work of a prophet as it is seen in these four men.

7

THE PROPHETS: PART 3, THE PROPHETS OF DESTRUCTION AND RECONSTRUCTION

THIS THIRD GROUP OF PROPHETS, dating from about 650 B.C. to 500 B.C., includes Zephaniah, Nahum, Habakkuk, Jeremiah, Ezekiel, Haggai, and Zechariah. Chapters 40-55 of the Book of Isaiah, as shown by the references to Cyrus, also deal with the latter part of this period. With this group of prophets, prophecy came to its climax. It then began to disappear with the passing of the kingdom, not to appear again until John the Baptist. These prophets saw one of the great turning points in the political history of the world, one which produced profound changes in the religious life of the Jews.

Speaking of the coming of Cyrus the Great and of his building a new and different empire, God declared, "Behold, I am doing a new thing" (Isa. 43:19). This is a key text to keep in mind for this changing epoch. At this crisis God seems to have come to the climax of his method of revelation through the Hebrew prophets. Jeremiah is the deepest, richest personality among the prophets, a climactic character. In the Book of Jeremiah there is recorded the promise of the New Covenant. "Behold, the days are coming, says the Lord, when I will make a new covenant with the house of Israel and with the house of Judah" (Jer. 31:31). That was God's assurance that he was doing a new thing in Israel. This group of prophets participated in the series of crises leading up to the great crisis of 538 B.C., the return from Exile, and the beginning of the new day.

1. THE PERIOD OF THESE PROPHETS OF DESTRUCTION AND RECONSTRUCTION

The period from about 650 B.C. to 500 B.C. was a watershed in Old Testament history. Crisis after crisis produced profound changes. By 650 B.C. the Assyrian Empire had reached the peak of its power and was entering upon its decay. In 612 B.C. the city of Nineveh, the glorious capital of Assyria, was destroyed and the Assyrian power came to an end. In 603 B.C. the Chaldeans under Nebuchadnezzar established themselves in world dominance in Babylon. In turn there came the decay and destruction of this ruthless power in 539 B.C. At that time a new period was inaugurated by Cyrus the Great. His conquest of the world marked one of the most definite changes history recounts.

During the hundred and fifty years from 650 B.C. to 500 B.C. the Jews went through severe tragedies. As Assyria grew weaker, Josiah asserted his freedom, reformed his kingdom, and enjoyed a brief period of prosperity. But the change was not deep enough and the times were too severe for the prosperity to be permanent. Read 2 Kings 22:1–23:37. Josiah's life ended in tragedy in 608 B.C. By 603 B.C. the new Babylonian, that is to say, the Chaldean, Empire ruled over Jerusalem. In 597 B.C. Nebuchadnezzar deported the best of the population of Jerusalem. In 586 B.C. he destroyed the city and deported another group. The kingdom of Judah was done for. See 2 Kings 24-25.

For two generations the Jewish people were exiles in Babylon or were scattered in other lands far and wide, except for a group of peasants in Judah who were constantly harassed by surrounding tribes. Then there appeared in history a new character, Cyrus. A new world empire was established, humane in its rule. Whereas the Assyrians and Babylonians had been ruthless, Cyrus permitted the Jews to return to Jerusalem and rebuild their Temple. This was an exceedingly difficult task, a challenge to faith. The new start was made despite extremely poor economic conditions. It was begun and continued only through the urging of the prophets, Haggai and Zechariah. Finally, by 515 B.C., the Second Temple was completed and the new religious community under the high priests made its beginning. Such was the period of ups and downs, of repeated tragedies, during this century and a half. The prophets had a most difficult task.

The events and persons of this period can be seen in the following time line. Note that Isaiah, Chapters 40-55, deals with this period. In these chapters the victorious career of Cyrus is celebrated (Isa. 45:1-7), and the exiles are summoned to go forth from Babylon, to flee from the Chaldeans (Isa. 43:14; 52:11-12). The destruction of Babylon is dramatically heralded (Isa. 47:1-15).

2. ZEPHANIAH, NAHUM, HABAKKUK

These three prophets belong to the period of the end of the Assyrian world empire and the beginning of the Chaldean (Babylonian). Zephaniah proclaimed the terrible days that were coming with the breakdown of Assyria under the attacks of the Scythians. These Scythians were wild marauding tribes from the north who, due to Assyria's increasing weakness, devastated lands far and wide. His is a solemn book in the midst of the trying times about 630-622 B.C. Nahum celebrated the fall of the city of Nineveh, that proud capital of the ruthless Assyrians who had won the hatred of all the people they had conquered and exploited. In 603 B.C. Habakkuk spoke out of a troubled mind, perplexed by the cruel Chaldeans as they came into power. Jeremiah's early ministry was in the same period as that of Zephaniah, Nahum, and Habakkuk. It was a most perplexing, confusing, ominous, discouraging time. But these men proclaimed the word of the God of Israel, the God of justice, who would surely carry out his work of righteousness.

3. THE BOOK OF DEUTERONOMY

Although Deuteronomy is not one of the books of prophecy, it had such an important part in the period that it should be noted here. In 2 Kings 22:1—23:30 is related the story of the finding of this book in the storehouse of the Temple and of the reformation it produced under Josiah. It is in Deuteronomy that the laws are found which

Josiah put into effect so rigorously. Deuteronomy is a book of wholehearted devotion to Yahweh, the God of Israel, and this is the theme of the prophets. Deuteronomy 6:4-9, called the *Shema,* is lesson number one for every pupil of the Old Testament: "Hear, O Israel: the Lord [Yahweh] our God is one Lord [Yahweh]; and you shall love the Lord [Yahweh] your God with all your heart, and with all your soul, and with all your might." But the reformation under Josiah ended with his death in 608 B.C. His sons reverted to the old pagan concept of the kingship and the nation fell to a low level. The Book of Deuteronomy furnished for this period the needed reforms. If they had been continued, the history of Judah would have been very different. This book of laws should be kept in mind when studying the prophets of this period. Although Josiah's reformation failed, the Book of Deuteronomy continued to be a great influence. It is a moving appeal to the true worship of the one God.

4. THE BOOK OF THE PROPHECIES OF JEREMIAH

Jeremiah is in many respects the greatest person with whom we can become acquainted in the Old Testament. He is not well known to Bible readers. This is regrettable but understandable. The Book of Jeremiah is not easy to read. His story is not told in an orderly way. Furthermore, he has the misfortune of being called "the weeping prophet," the writer of Lamentations. This reputation misrepresents Jeremiah. The study of this deep, inward person in his profound experience of God is one of the most enriching blessings offered in the Old Testament. In the short space of this lesson, Jeremiah can only be introduced. He rewards more study.

Look first at the book as a book. It is one of the larger rolls, fifty-two chapters. There are four parts: 1. The words of Jeremiah (chaps. 1-25). 2. The story of Jeremiah written by his faithful friend, Baruch (chaps. 26-45). 3. A collection of oracles regarding various kingdoms (chaps. 46-51). 4. A historical appendix (chap. 52). Thus, the book is a collection of collections which gives large blocks of the message of Jeremiah, but makes no effort to recount his story completely and in order. Yet in the book itself the main facts can be discovered, and through them we can become acquainted with this searcher of the deepest truth of communion with God.

In brief, this is the story of Jeremiah. His home was in the village of Anathoth, a short distance north of Jerusalem. He came from an old priestly family which was no longer in favor with the high priestly families of the Temple. His writings show a man of deep feelings, tender, excitable even to great heat, a lyric poet of rare ability, a lover of the quiet life of the village. By nature he was retiring and had no desire for a public career with all its strain and stress. Upon this sensitive soul there fell all the tragedies of the national and world upheavals from 626 B.C. to 586 B.C.

These struck the young Jeremiah first in the threat of the advancing hordes of Scythians who were devastating the falling Assyrian Empire. His deep feelings are shown in his poems found in chapters 2:1—6:30. He reacted as only a deep lover of his people could and gave his message in moving poetry. After this came the vigorous and rigorous reformation under Josiah in 622 B.C. Jeremiah entered this as a teacher of the covenant. But the reformation collapsed with the death of Josiah in 608 B.C. Then Jeremiah was called upon to face the new rulers (Jehoahaz, Jehoiakim, Jehoiakin, and Zedekiah)—men who had turned away from worshiping the Lord with all their hearts, with all their souls, and with all their might (Deut. 6:4). These

rulers turned rather to political intrigues, the struggle for
power, and the debased worship of the baals. From 608
B.C. to 586 B.C. the nation hastened along the way of decay
and destruction.

Nebuchadnezzar, the Chaldean, by the battle of Car-
chemish, 603 B.C., established the New Babylonian world
empire. The kings of Judah schemed, plotted, shifted poli-
cies, changed from pro-Chaldean to pro-Egyptian and back
again, got into trouble after trouble, never seemed to learn
anything. Jeremiah stood alone amid all these ups and
downs, the object of suspicion, of hatred, a man of sorrows
and acquainted with grief. His message was twofold:
"Amend your ways" and "Accept the Chaldeans as the
present world rulers." This made him the most unpopular
man in Jerusalem. He was persecuted, imprisoned, thrown
into a well. But Jeremiah persevered in giving his message. In 596 B.C. the Chaldeans deported the best of the
population. Finally, in 586 B.C., they destroyed both the
city of Jerusalem and the Temple. So the kingdom of
Judah was brought to an end. Jeremiah chose to stay in
the ruined land, but rebels carried him away to Egypt where
he died.

In chapters 7-10 is the great Temple Sermon. In chapter
26 is an account of this event. As Amos had stood at the
gate of the royal sanctuary in Bethel and pronounced the
word of God, so Jeremiah stood at the gate of the Temple
in Jerusalem and spoke as God commanded him. "Amend
your ways and your doings, and I will dwell in this place.
Do not trust in these deceptive words: 'This is the temple
of the Lord, the temple of the Lord, the temple of the
Lord'" (Jer. 7:3-4). The king and the lords put on a great
show at the Temple sacrifices which Jeremiah thoroughly
condemned. "For in the day that I brought them out of
the land of Egypt, I did not speak to your fathers or com-

mand them concerning burnt offerings and sacrifices. But
this command I gave them, 'Obey my voice, and I will
be your God, and you shall be my people; and walk in all
the way that I command you, that it may be well with
you'" (Jer. 7:22-23). (See also Amos 5:21-25; Hos. 6:6;
Isa. 1:11-17; Mic. 6:6-8; Ps. 51:16-17; Matt. 9:13; 12:7).
In Jeremiah, chap. 26, the excitement caused by this ser
mon is very clear. It almost cost Jeremiah his life. Only
the intervention of his friends saved him. This sermon
gives the heart of Jeremiah's message to the evil rulers
who finally brought about the destruction of the kingdom.
As with the other prophets, it was Jeremiah's function to
tell the nation the nature of the true service of God and
to warn the people of the inevitable end of their iniquity.
"I will do to the house . . . as I did to Shiloh" (Jer. 7:14).
And this, God did. In 586 B.C. the Temple was destroyed,
house and altar alike.

But like the other prophets, Jeremiah was a messenger
of hope. In Jeremiah 31:31-34 is the most penetrating
promise in the Old Testament. It is the most deeply religious promise, for it deals with conversion and the new
birth, although these terms are not used. "I will make a
new covenant." "I will put my law within them, and I
will write it upon their hearts." "I will forgive their iniquity,
and I will remember their sin no more." These three
statements are God's solemn assurance given through Jeremiah. God binds himself and his people in a binding
covenant. He will do his part and they must do theirs.
God promises to write his law in the heart and mind so
that it will become an inward law, a deep personal commitment. God promises that he will do this through forgiveness of sins. The evil rulers and the sinful people were
carrying the kingdom down to ruin. Iniquity, bringing
punishment, was the terrible fact. But in that darkest hour

Jeremiah spoke God's most gracious promise. This severest condemner of Israel, the one who suffered most at the hands of his opponents, had the clearest vision of God's purpose for the true Israel.

5. THE BOOK OF THE PROPHECIES OF EZEKIEL

Ezekiel, a younger contemporary of Jeremiah, was a member of the Jerusalem priesthood, the aristocracy of the priests. As a young man he had been carried into captivity in the first deportation. From 597 B.C. to 570 B.C. he lived among the exiles and shared all their fears and hopes. He is called the Pastor of the Exiles. See Ezekiel 3:14-21. Entering into all their perplexities and understanding all their wrong ideas, he gave himself fully to these captives, advising, warning, comforting, and inspiring them. From 597 B.C. to 586 B.C. he spoke warnings of the coming destruction of Jerusalem which would follow upon the evil ways of the rulers. From 586 B.C. to 570 B.C. he brought to the discouraged exiles his inspiring vision of a new and divinely glorified Jerusalem.

The Jews were living in the midst of the impressive city of Babylon with all its kingly glory and the elaborate worship of its gods, especially their chief deity, Maruk. Outwardly it seemed to the Chaldeans and the people whom the Chaldeans had conquered that Marduk was the lord of lords, the god of gods. The God of Israel seemed to be defeated and left with no tokens of prestige or power. The people of this seemingly discredited god sank into hopelessness. They believed that their fathers had sinned and that they, the children, were suffering a punishment not due them (chap. 18). They felt that they were like a valley full of dead bones and that they would never come to life again (chap. 37). How to warn and encourage the exiles was the task which caused Ezekiel "bitterness in the heat of [his] spirit" (Ezek. 3:14). He suffered with and for his people in their time of despair.

The Book of Ezekiel is rather difficult reading. His mind worked in elaborate visions (see Ezek. 1:1-28) or in elaborate architectural plans (see Ezek. 40:1—48:35). But there are four facts in his message which are central in the messages of all of these prophets. Ezekiel preached these facts, however, in his own unique way. These four facts are the glory of Yahweh, the forgiveness of sins, the new birth of the nation, and the new Jerusalem. These teachings will be considered in turn.

(a) The Glory of Yahweh. In Ezekiel's day the gods of the other nations seemed very real, especially Marduk. This great god of the world-ruling city of Babylon seemed the mightiest of all the gods. For Israel in that day, it was Marduk versus Yahweh, the god of the Chaldeans versus the God of Israel. With the destruction of Jerusalem, Yahweh seemed deprived of all glory. To other peoples he was a negligible deity, for his people had been enslaved and his temple had been overthrown. The most difficult task for Ezekiel was the awakening in Israel of a strong conviction of the glory of Yahweh. Chapter 1 is strange, puzzling, and confusing at first reading. It is a word picture of the chariot-throne of Yahweh which moves by the indwelling Spirit. The four figures which sustain it have the faces of an ox, a lion, an eagle, and a man. These are the representations of the four chief gods of Babylon: Ox for Marduk, Lion for Nergal, Eagle for Ninib, Man for Nabu. Thus Ezekiel is asserting the supremacy of the God of Israel and the nothingness of the great gods of Babylon.

(b) The Forgiveness of Sins (see chap. 18). The exiles felt that they were caught in the guilt of their fathers, for whose sin the kingdom had been destroyed. Ezekiel asserts that guilt belongs to the guilty, that the person who sins will surely die. This is that statement of individual guilt. The exiles did not need to be convinced about the dying, but they did need to know that whatever their fathers had done, they themselves could turn to the Lord and live. The soul that sinned, *it* shall die, not another. This verse must be read with the emphasis where Ezekiel placed it. "If a wicked man turn away from all his sins . . . *he* shall surely live; *he* shall not die." Here is the assurance of the possibility of the forgiveness of sin to a generation in bitter despair because of the sins of the previous generation.

(c) **The New Birth** (see chap. 37). The exiles were like a valley full of dead bones. As a nation, they were like the skeletons which covered the ground after an army had completed its slaughter. In this vision Ezekiel sees the dead nation given life again. "I will put my Spirit within you, and you shall live, and I will place you in your own land; then you shall know that I, the Lord [Yahweh], have spoken, and I have done it, says the Lord [Yahweh]" (Ezek. 37:14).

(d) **The New Jerusalem.** The old Jerusalem had been made a pile of ruins. In its place, Ezekiel pictures in vision a new Jerusalem with a new temple and a new organization. In chapters 40-48, Ezekiel writes like a city-planner and like an architect drawing the specifications of a new community. His account presents an elaborate plan which could not be carried out just as he describes it, but his message is clear. God would bring his people back to their land, and there could be a new, rightly organized city of God's people. "And the name of the city henceforth shall be, The Lord is there," or, as it is in Hebrew, "Yahweh-Shammah" (Ezek. 48:35).

So Ezekiel, up to 570 B.C., nourished the flickering spirit of discouraged Israel. One of his assurances (Ezek. 34:26) has passed over into a familiar gospel song: "There shall be showers of blessing." In that song something of the spirit of Ezekiel continues within the church.

6. ISAIAH, CHAPTERS 40-55

These beautiful evangelistic chapters deal with the period of Cyrus' triumphant advance against Babylon and of the release of such exiles as desired to return to Jerusalem to rebuild the Temple. Chapter 45:1-7 is written as a proclamation addressed to Cyrus. He is called "the Lord's anointed." His commission is for the sake of Israel. This ruler was a new and better force in the ancient world. In a few years he made a conquest of the world greater than that of any of his predecessors. In 550 B.C. he became king of Persia; in 546 B.C. he defeated Croesus in Asia Minor; in 539 B.C. he captured Babylon. It took him only about a decade "to subdue nations before him and ungird the loins of kings, to open doors before him that gates may not be closed" (Isa. 45:1). His conquest was constructive, not destructive. Cyrus opened a new day. Recall Isaiah 43:19: "Behold, I am doing a new thing." So said the Lord in the midst of the new day brought in by Cyrus.

Between the end of Isaiah, chapter 39, and the beginning of chapter 40, there is a century and a half of time. Chapter 39 deals with an event in 701 B.C. Cyrus advanced on Babylon in 539 B.C. By that date the situation had changed completely in Israel and in the whole world. Chapter 40 opens with the word "Comfort." What a change from Amos', "Woe to you who desire the day of the Lord!" (Amos 5:18), or the series of "Woes" in Isaiah 5:8-23! Isaiah 40-55 is addressed to the down-and-out, discouraged exiles in their utter weakness after two generations of sufferings. They needed comfort, reassurance, an evangelistic revival. Compare Ezekiel 37. Hence, these chapters are an enthusiastic message of good news, calling Israel to life again, to depart from Babylon with singing and joy, to begin a new day in their own land. These chapters overflow with songs, real gospel songs. Prophecy stands at its highest in this evangel.

Chapters 40-55 should be read as a unit—read as a magnificent poem in which a herald announces to the down-and-out nation that God is doing a new thing, that the redemption of Israel is close at hand by the power of God, through the instrumentality of Cyrus, and that Israel is summoned to be the servant of God in bringing salvation to the whole world. This large unit begins and ends with gracious invitation. Isaiah 40 is a familiar and stirring summons, "Comfort, comfort my people," and Isaiah 55 is another urgent call, "Ho, every one who thirsts, come to the waters." The whole gospel message is bracketed by these invitations. They express the pervading spirit of the gracious call.

The following outline will help in reading this portion of the Book of Isaiah:

I. Prologue: The coming of the Lord (40:1-11).
II. The Incomparable Greatness of the Lord [Yahweh] (40:12 —41:29).
III. Israel, the Servant of the Lord and the Work of Redemption (42:1—44:23).
IV. Through Cyrus, the Lord [Yahweh], the One and Only God, Will Overthrow Bablyon, Redeem Israel, Estabish His Sole Sovereignty, and Become the Salvation of the Whole World (44:24—48:22).
V. The Splendid Future of Israel; the Redemptive Sufferings of the Servant (49:1—54:17).
VI. Epilogue: The Lord's Gracious Invitation to Salvation (55: 1-13).

The primary teaching of these chapters is that Yahweh (that is, God as known by Moses and the prophets, the God of loving-kindness, steadfast love, justice and redemptive grace) is the one and only God. This is stated time after time. It is emphasized with strongest urgency and persuasion, as of one speaking to a people who did not see and accept this fact. In one sense, this is counter-propaganda, because in Babylon the Chaldeans worshiped Marduk as the supreme god and a whole company of lesser gods under him.

In our English versions much of the force of the original is lost through the use of the word "Lord" where the Hebrew has "Yahweh." Consider these passages: "I am Yahweh, that is my name" (Isa. 42.8). This is translated "I am the Lord, that is my name." "Before me no god was formed, nor shall there be any after me. I, I am the Lord [Yahweh] and besides me there is no savior" (Isa. 43:10-11). "Thus says the Lord [Yahweh], the King of Israel and his Redeemer, the Lord of hosts: 'I am the first and I am the last; besides me there is no god'" (Isa. 44:6). "I am the Lord [Yahweh] and there is no other, besides me there is no God" (Isa. 45:5). "There is no other god besides me, a righteous God and a Savior; there is none besides me. Turn to me and be saved, all the ends of the earth! For I am God, and there is no other" (Isa. 45:21-22). These and other statements in Isaiah 40-55 are the greatest teachings about the one and only God. This is not the philosophy which we call monotheism, but the gospel of the one Savior for Israel and for all the ends of the earth, one God, one World, one Salvation. There could be a new start for the nation only through enthusiastic devotion to the One True God. In contrast, see the sarcastic words regarding idols (Isa. 40:18-20; 41:6-7).

The second main theme is Israel, the Servant of the One and Only God. The word "servant" is characteristic of these chapters. The prophecy is more than a call to Israel to come out of exile. Israel is called to become the servant of the Lord and to perform his work. This is repeatedly

stated. Why should Israel be called out of its death, the
death which came by reason of her iniquity? Why should
a nation which had failed miserably be called into life
again? In the first instance, God had called Abraham and
his family that he might bless them and make them a blessing (Gen. 12:1-3; K.J. and A.S.V.). Now, in doing a new
thing, God again called Israel out of bondage with the
emphasis upon being his servant to the ends of the earth.
That could be the only justification of Israel's redemption
from her sin and failure. Read Isaiah 41:8-9; 42:1, 19;
43:10; 44:1-2, 21; 44:26; 45:4; 48:20; 49:3, 5-7; 50:10.
These are significant passages.

See how frequently the prophet uses this term "servant"
in trying to awaken the discouraged people to a deeper
idea of the meaning of being the chosen people. Especially
important is Isaiah 49:6: " 'It is too light a thing that
you should be my servant to raise up the tribes of Jacob
and to restore the preserved of Israel; I will give you as
a light to the nations, that my salvation may reach to the
end of the earth.' " "A light to the nations" is a key phrase.
This contains the meaning of the evangel to the exiles.
The religion of the Old Testament in its deepest truth is
missionary. That is what "servant" means.

Then there is the supreme Servant passage, Isaiah 52:13
—53:12. The break in our English translation between
chapter 52 and chapter 53 is unfortunate. The passage
begins at 52:13 and is incomplete without its introduction. Here the Servant is the vicarious sufferer who through
his suffering brings salvation to the nations. These chapters which call Israel to be "my servant" leap up beyond
Israel to that Servant who is found only in Jesus Christ.
Isaiah 52:13—53:12 is an impassioned effort to lift Israel
into the vision of the Suffering Servant, the Savior of the
World.

Chapters 40-55 should be read through in their entirety in the spirit of the heraldic prophet. "Get you up on a high mountain, O Zion, herald of good tidings; lift up your voice with strength, O Jerusalem, herald of good tidings; lift it up, fear not; say to the cities of Judah, 'Behold your God'" (Isa. 40:9). The prophets spoke directly to the people. In them God addressed the nation. Only with a lively sense of the people being addressed in their changing feelings of fear and hope can the prophecies be felt. Only with a lively sense of the speaker as he uses threat, comfort, and promise, can the prophecies become living. It is in this manner that they should be read aloud, in large sections, as spoken, vital, moving words. From the literary standpoint there is no greater example of persuasive speech than that which we have in Isaiah 40-55. God used a gifted prophet who can lift the mind into lofty communication with God, if we enter into these words in their own vitality of inspiration. By these enthusiastic messages new hope was awakened in down-and-out Israel.

7. HAGGAI AND ZECHARIAH

These two prophets worked together during the years 520 B.C. to 515 B.C. to accomplish the building of the Second Temple. The edict of Cyrus, recorded in Ezra 1:2-4, gave permission to "rebuild the house of the Lord, the God of Israel," and "everyone whose spirit God had stirred to go up to rebuild the house of the Lord which is in Jerusalem" came up out of captivity. This was in 538 B.C. When they arrived at the ruined city and the devastated land of Judah, the immediate, practical problems of making a living from the soil engaged their energies. They did at once "build the altar of the God of Israel, to offer burnt offerings upon it, as it is written in the law of Moses the man of God. They set the altar in its place" (Ezra

3:2-3), and they began plans for the Temple. The builders laid the foundations (Ezra 3:6-13). But adversaries opposed the work (Ezra 4:1-24). Also the work of making new homes absorbed the time and energies of the people. "Then the work on the house of God which is in Jerusalem stopped; and it ceased until the second year of the reign of Darius King of Persia (Ezra 4:24; 5:1; Hag. 1:1; Zech. 1:1). These two men were revivalists. They "prophesied to the Jews"; that is, they stirred the people by their inspiration to resume the building of the Temple and revived them as often as they grew lax. We can follow their work step by step, month by month, year by year, from August, 520, to March, 515:

1. The appeal to begin, Aug., 520 (Hag. 1:1-11).
2. The work begun, Sept. 520 (Hag. 1:12-15).
3. The second appeal, Oct., 520 (Hag. 2:1-9).
4. A call to return to the Lord, Nov., 520 (Zech. 1:1-6).
5. The cornerstone laid, Dec., 520 (Hag. 2:10-23).
6. Visions to stimulate the work, Feb., 519 (Zech. 1:7—6:15).
7. Promises of prosperity, Dec., 518 (Zech. 7:1—8:23).
8. The completion of the Temple, March, 515 (Ezra 6:15).

So the Second Temple, which continued in use down to the time of Herod, provided for the ritual observances of Israel as stated in the Law. The life of Israel was concentrated in this sanctuary with its continual burnt offering morning and evening, and the three annual celebrations of each year: the Passover, the Feast of Weeks, and the Feast of Tabernacles (Ex. 23:14). Especially important was the Day of Atonement. This sacred ceremony is fully described in Leviticus, chapter 16. The high priest became the leading official in Jerusalem. Persia allowed no king, so there developed a high priestly aristocracy of the house of Zadok, the Sadducees of the New Testament. The prophets soon disappeared from Israel.

Other prophets of this late period should be noted. Joel, in a time of drought and locusts, pronounced the day of the Lord, called for national repentance, and promised the outpouring of the Spirit of God upon all flesh. Obadiah with impassioned severity condemned Edom for its spoliation of Judah in the day of calamity. Malachi (the name means "my messenger") condemned Israel as a cheat who had despised and polluted the name of God. His book closes with the glorious promises of the way of redemption, which is a fitting conclusion for the entire Old Testament.

The Book of Jonah is a strange writing among the other books of the prophets. It is a penetrating charge against a self-centered nation which had closed its mind against its mission to the Gentiles. It is a moving declaration of God's compassion for all peoples and even for the animals.

The Hebrew prophets were men into whom the Spirit of God entered, giving them insight into his word. These men, out of their insight, spoke regarding the past, the present, and the future, for the purpose of God is one, and his character is always the same. The prophets spoke of the loving-kindness, righteousness, and justice of the covenanted God of Israel in the past, the present, and the future; they presented him as the Creator of heaven and earth, the Savior of all flesh.

8

THE SCHOOLING OF THE CHOSEN PEOPLE

THE TITLE OF THIS CHAPTER might well be used to characterize the entire Old Testament, for the Old Testament gives a remarkable account of how God chose a particular people and disciplined them for his gracious purposes. From the point of view of the Old Testament, to be the elect people did not mean special merit or favor, but special responsibility. For this stewardship, the chosen people needed discipline. To the task of disciplining them, God gave himself with divine persistence.

There is a statement in Jeremiah 7:25-26 which shows this patient work of God in spite of Israel's resistance: "From the day that your fathers came out of the land of Egypt to this day, I have persistently sent all my servants the prophets to them, day after day; yet they did not listen to me, or incline their heart, but stiffened their neck." (Compare Amos 2:10-12.) These verses summarize the story. They reveal God at work. God is an industrious, persistent worker. The King James Version gives this picturesque rendering: "I have sent unto you all my servants the prophets, daily rising up early and sending them." The people, however, were inattentive, stiff-necked, and forgetful. Because they did not learn their lessons, they got into disaster after disaster. But God kept at his work. He persisted in sending messengers to them. In this lesson we shall see one of the most important and fruitful points of this instruction. God put his people in school. Ezra, the Scribe, the Teacher, made the chosen people a nation of students well instructed in the Law; and Nehemiah organized their life as a city without reproach by building its walls and teaching the people how to live in co-operative citizenship.

1. "THE FEEBLE JEWS"

An enemy so described Israel in the days of Ezra and Nehemiah. Beneath the hatred and scorn of these words was a certain amount of fact. The recovery after the exile had been slow and discouraging. The Jews—that is, that section of the Hebrews who were of Judah—were a small and insignificant people, limited to an area no more than twenty miles square which had been badly devastated by war. As to outward circumstances, therefore, "the feeble Jews" was a correct description.

There were three distinct phases in the early postexilic period.

> (1) 538 B.C. to 515 B.C. The first return, the building of the altar, and the Temple. Leaders: Zerubbabel and Joshua, Haggai and Zechariah. This phase, covering a quarter of a century, is related in Ezra 1:1—6:22.
> (2) 515 B.C. to 458 B.C. No record. No leaders of distinction. A half-century of slump, feebleness, and threat of disintegration.
> (3) 458 B.C. to 432 B.C. Building the city walls, establishing the teaching of the Law and organizing the life of the city. Leaders, Ezra and Nehemiah. This phase, covering a quarter of a century, is related in Ezra 7:1—10:44 and in the Book of Nehemiah.

The account of the work of Ezra begins at Ezra 7:1. The first six chapters of the Book of Ezra deal with the period from 538 B.C., the date of the return from captivity, to

515 B.C., the date of the completion of the rebuilding of the Temple. Ezra came to Jerusalem in 458 B.C. His coming is spoken of as a second return from the exile. From 538 B.C. to 458 B.C. the Jews experienced hard times in the devastated land of Judah. The country was open to the inroads of Samaritans, Ammonites, Edomites, and other surrounding peoples. The city of Jerusalem had no wall and hence was exposed to any foe. The citizens were suffering economically and were disorganized in their religious practices and ideas. Two of their worst enemies expressed their contempt for the Jews in this way: "Now when Sanballat heard that we were building the wall, he was angry and greatly enraged, and he ridiculed the Jews. And he said in the presence of his brethren and of the army of Samaria 'What are these feeble Jews doing? Will they restore things? Will they sacrifice? Will they finish up in a day? Will they revive the stones out of the heaps of rubbish, and burned ones at that?' Tobiah the Ammonite was by him and he said, 'Yes, what are they building— if a fox goes up on it he will break down their stone wall'" (Neh. 4:1-3). So feeble did the Jews seem!

In Ezra 9:5-15, Ezra records the prayer he made when he came to Jerusalem. It shows how bad conditions were. Ezra was called at a time when the chosen people, humanly speaking, were about to become as heathen as were the surrounding peoples. They were few in number, feeble in power, with no political standing. Judah and the surrounding area were a small county in the midst of the mighty Persian Empire. There was no king, no governor in Israel. When they first returned, their leaders were Zerubbabel, of the house of David, and Joshua, the head of the priests (Ezra 3:2; Haggai 1:1). But there was no place for a royal prince under the Persian rule. Zerubbabel disappears from the records, leaving Joshua, the priest, as the head of the nation.

Ezra and Nehemiah were called to a weak, discouraged nation about to go out of existence.

2. EZRA THE SCRIBE

Ezra is introduced in Ezra 7:1. He belonged to the high priestly aristocracy. His family tree carries his ancestry back to the great names of Zadok and Aaron. This gave him high standing. He is thus described: "He was a scribe skilled in the law of Moses" (Ezra 7:6). Much is said in that statement. A scribe was, first of all, a skilled copyist. All writing was done by hand. To copy the ancient scrolls with scrupulous exactness required the discipline of a trained scholar. Furthermore, the scribe was expert in the knowledge of the Law; thus, he could instruct others and judge cases. The scribe was a scholar, lawyer, and teacher. In terms of our day, Ezra would have been worthy of the degree of Doctor of Divinity. This made Ezra an outstanding individual, the best educated person among the Jews. "Ezra had set his heart to study the law of the Lord, and to do it, and to teach his statutes and ordinances in Israel" (Ezra 7:10). He was a dedicated servant of God. "You are sent by the king and his seven counselors to make inquiries about Judah and Jerusalem according to the law of your God, which is in your hand" (Ezra 7:14).

A picture of Ezra should show him with the scroll of the Law in his hand, the scroll he had written, that he might study it, do it, and teach it. Ezra is always called "the scribe" (see Ezra 7:21, 25; Neh. 8:1, 9, 13). He is the first of the rabbis. In Ezra, the scribe takes the place of the prophet.

3. EZRA'S EARLY WORK IN JERUSALEM

In Ezra 9:1—10:44 the beginning of Ezra's work in Jerusalem is recounted. He had to deal with the problem of mixed marriages, for such marriages involved mixed religions. It required severity of action to demand the putting away of foreign wives. But it was a time of crisis when this drastic major operation seemed necessary for the well-being of the nation. Ezra faced the problem with the seriousness of his whole-souled commitment to God. The Book of Ruth with its story of a foreign wife, Ruth the Moabitess, is relevant to the situation and shows another side of the question, namely, the conversion of a foreign woman, an Edomite.

4. EZRA TEACHES THE LAW

The great work of Ezra occurred late in 444 B.C. (see Neh. 8:1-18). After some years of teaching the Law, the time was ripe for a great day of consecration. "All the people gathered as one man into the square before the Water Gate; and they told Ezra the scribe to bring the book of the law of Moses which the Lord had given to Israel." Ezra had become known as the authoritative scribe and had so far taught the people that they were ready to accept the Law. So he read from it "from early morning until midday, in the presence of the men and the women and those who could understand; and the ears of all the people were attentive to the book of the law," and certain men "helped the people to understand the law . . . And they read from the book, from the law of God, clearly; and they gave the sense, so that the people understood the reading."

The next day they "came together to Ezra the scribe in order to study the words of the law." In that great day Ezra made the Jews students of the Law. He introduced the discipline of careful, systematic instruction for all the people, high and low, men and women, adults and children. Ezra gave the nation a textbook, i.e., the scroll that was in his hand, consisting of the Law of Moses which God had

given to Israel. Now there was a very definite way by which
the chosen people could be trained.

Ezra brought the Jews of his day to a serious commitment, a commitment which all of the people understood
and fully accepted. No such commitment had been made
previous to this. Thorough instruction, repeated instruction,
powerful prayer, impressive ceremony—all were used to
deepen this formation of purpose in the nation as a whole.
Its success shows it to have been one of the most significant
acts in the world's history. Ezra was the Second Lawgiver.
Ezra made the Jews a nation of students and observers of
the Law. From his day forward, wherever the Jews went
they carried the Law and diligently studied it. They carried out the injunction of the *Shema* (Deut. 6:6-19). On
the importance of the *Shema,* see pages 52-53.

5. NEHEMIAH THE COURT OFFICIAL

Often in the Old Testament God worked through teams
of men: Moses and Aaron; Elijah and Elisha; Amos, Hosea,
Micah, Isaiah; Jeremiah and Ezekiel; Haggai and Zechariah;
Ezra and Nehemiah. Likewise, we find that persons of
different gifts were needed to carry on the many-sided
work of God. Ezra the Scribe could perform one phase
of the work needed in the day of the weakness of the
Jews. But he was capable only in his line. Another was
called for a task just as necessary as that which Ezra carried through. This leader was Nehemiah. In the Book of
Nehemiah 1:1—2:8, Nehemiah records his own story. He
appears as a capable court official of high rank under
Artaxerxes, King of Persia. This was Artaxerxes I, 464-
424 B.C. To sit in the presence of the king at the royal
table and to taste the wine before the king indicates a high
appreciation of Nehemiah's services, character, and good
company. When this cupbearer asked to be sent to Jeru-

salem to rebuild its walls, the king displayed perfect confidence in his friend. So Nehemiah was sent to the land of Judah to serve as the governor of the city, which he was commissioned to restore. From 586 B.C. to 444 B.C., a period of almost a century and a half, the walls of the city and many of its buildings had been rubble. It was not so much a city as a place to be despised and overrun. Nehemiah had a difficult task both with those within the city and the various opponents outside. But he persisted in his efforts to make Jerusalem a city without reproach.

6. THE WORK OF NEHEMIAH

Nehemiah carefully surveyed his task and then secured remarkable teamwork in getting the walls built. This is related in detail in Nehemiah 2:11—3:6. Nehemiah's skill in supervising the work is evident in the closing statement of the account: "So we built the wall; and the wall was joined together to half its height. For the people had a mind to work" (Neh. 4:6).

This was achieved in the face of opposing leaders who employed every trick of threat and persuasion against Nehemiah (see Neh. 4:7-23; 6:1-14). Sanballat, Tobiah, and Gershem, foes from Samaria, Ammon, and Arabia, plotted against Nehemiah. They tried scheme after scheme, but failed. Nehemiah's reply to their invitation to meet with them in one of the villages shows his consecrated spirit: "I am doing a great work and I cannot come down" (Neh. 6:3).

Nehemiah had to organize the city government and to build up its population (Neh. 7:1-73). Also he had to deal with the problem of usury (Neh. 5:1-19), and make provision for the Temple services (Neh. 12:44-47). It was through this wise and forceful administration that Nehemiah made Jerusalem again a real city.

Because of Nehemiah's work, the Jews at long last had a city in which they could carry on their life and their sacred institutions according to the Law. They had a special destiny to serve which had been endangered by the disorganization of the old ruined city. Nehemiah accomplished the work because he planned wisely, was incorruptible, and had the skill to get the citizens of Jerusalem to co-operate in building the walls and reorganizing the life of the city. With Ezra he made Jerusalem a city which was aware of the stewardship of the chosen people.

7. THE SYNAGOGUE

Just when the synagogue began we do not know. The Old Testament tells us nothing about it. But in connection with Ezra and the teaching of the Law, it should be mentioned. Ezra's work required scribes, the regular reading of the Law, and the systematic teaching of children. The synagogue was the response to that need. It was a local institution. It was democratic, for all were alike before God. It was a place of worship where the Law and the Prophets were read and interpreted. The Book of Psalms furnished for it the prayers and hymns which make for true worship. The Jews went forth into the world with the synagogue, organizing one wherever there were a few heads of families. In the synagogue the Gentiles heard the teaching of One God, perfect in holiness, abounding in loving-kindness, establishing justice, and calling upon all people to worship God according to God's true nature. So the Jews became a light to the nations and prepared the way for the coming of the church.

9

THE OLD TESTAMENT COMPLETED

GOD TOOK A LONG TIME in the making of the Old Testament. He caused it to grow through many centuries, many situations, many crises, many men. "First the blade, then the ear, then the full grain in the ear" (Mark 4:28). At last, in the fullness of God's work, the Old Testament was completed in the form in which we have it, and it was sent into the world to perform its work in accordance with God's purpose.

There is no definite date which can be set for this completion. The end was not marked by any official body at any given date. But by the time of Jesus, and probably by 100 B.C., the canon of the Old Testament was set, and these various rolls were being taught in the synagogues far and wide throughout the Roman World.

The peculiar possession of the Jews was the Old Testament. The peculiar characteristic of the Jews was their zeal for these scriptures. The peculiar mission of the Jews was to collect these books, study them diligently, practice them scrupulously, and teach them constantly wherever they might be scattered. This gave the seedbed in which the church began. There are certain important facts to note regarding this period of the final assembling of these thirty-nine books. A knowledge of these facts will aid us in understanding certain of the late books.

114

1. TIMES OF TESTING

The welding of the various books into our sacred collection took place during the period when the chosen people were passing through a fiery furnace. The work of the Lord is often spoken of as being like a refiner's fire. Such were the centuries after the return from the exile. When the prophet summoned the Jews to leave Babylon, he promised God's help through the afflictions which awaited them.

"But now thus says the Lord,
    he who created you, O Jacob,
    he who formed you, O Israel:
'Fear not, for I have redeemed you;
    I have called you by name, you are mine.
When you pass through the waters I will be with you;
    and through the rivers, they shall not overwhelm you;
When you walk through fire you shall not be burned,
    and the flame shall not consume you'" (Isa. 43:1-2).

Such was the experience of God's people in the period of the completion of the Old Testament. They suffered under a succession of empires which time and again almost destroyed them. This is indicated in the following time line.

	639 B.C.		333 B.C.		63 B.C.	
CHALDEANS		PERSIANS		GREEKS		ROMANS

CHALDEANS	PERSIANS	GREEKS	ROMANS
Nebuchadnezzar	Cyrus	Alexander	Caesars
Belshazzar	Darius	The Ptolemies	
	Xerxes	(Kings of the South)	
	Artaxerxes	The Seleucids	
		(Kings of the North)	
		Antiochus IV	
		165 63	
		Maccabees	

Throughout this series of empires the Jews lived the life of the underdog; they were victims of rulers who were beastlike in their persecutions. The names of two Chaldean rulers were burned deep into their memories: Nebuchadnezzar, the destroyer of the Temple, and Belshazzar, the profane defiler of the vessels of the Temple. After the Persians, who became increasingly tyrannical, the swift-conquering Alexander brought the Jews under the dominance of Greek rulers. The Ptolemies in Egypt (the king of the south) and the Seleucids in Syria (the king of the north) fought back and forth for the control of Palestine. To the long-suffering Jews, the victims of these powers, these rulers were all alike in character, for they fought one another, spoiled kingdoms, put saints to death, defied the Most High. They were as beasts. Their victims felt the only proper symbols for these kingdoms were the ravenous beasts. In times of persecution, when care needed to be taken in talking about the rulers, the persecuted spoke about the lion, eagle (vulture), bear, leopard, wild goat, and the terrible dragon. They used these symbols rather than the names of the tyrants.

The Law, the Prophets, and the Writings, so different from the mind of these beastlike persons, became holy scriptures. These writings proved themselves to be the word of God when they sustained the faithful in the times of hardest testing. The persecuted clung to these books, not because of some argument in their defense, but because of their inherent power to sustain God's people in the midst of the fiery furnace of persecution. The various books were gathered, copied, and studied, because in them God spoke the word by which his people could live in spite of the triumphant power of the lion, eagle, bear, leopard, wild goat, or dragon.

The Old Testament has always proved to be the living,

sustaining word of God to any people passing through the waters of affliction or the flames of testing. Coming out of hard times, it helps men in hard times.

2. THE SEVEREST TESTING

The most critical period in the story of the completion of the Old Testament occurred when the power of this word of God to produce the endurance of the saints was tested during the awful persecution under Antiochus (168-165 B.C.). Although this event is not related in the Old Testament itself, some knowledge of it is of utmost importance in understanding the Old Testament in the final phases of its formation. This story should be read in 1 Maccabees, chap. 1 (cf., Daniel 11:21-39).

Antiochus IV was king of Syria, 175-164 B.C. He called himself Antiochus Epiphanes, which means God Manifest. Taking his claim to divinity seriously, he undertook to assert his power. In Daniel he is called the king of the north.

Antiochus was a shrewd, vain, and ambitious king. He was clever in all the tricks of power politics, and was without any scruples in the pursuit of his goal. He was, in the words of the Book of Daniel, a "big horn with the eyes of a man and a mouth speaking great things." From his father, Antiochus the Great, he had inherited the conceit of becoming a second Alexander. This totalitarian set about the task of making his kingdom one in Greek culture. His imperial order was that all his people should forsake their own religions and join in worshiping Zeus Olympius (Jupiter). When this decree came to the city of Jerusalem, to the place of the worship of the "Most High" (as the pious Jew designated the God of Israel), there was a division into two parties. In the priestly aristocracy, the house of Zadok, there were those who favored the new Greek ways and adopted them. The pious Jews, the saints, trained in the Law and the Prophets and zealously devoted to them, were uncompromising opponents of Antiochus. They resisted any worship except wholehearted devotion to the God of Israel, the Holy One, the Most High.

The greater the authoritarian pressure of the tyrant, the firmer was the resolve of the pious not to defile themselves. Theirs was the religion of the *Shema* (Deut. 6:6-9). Under the program of Antiochus, the Jews were to discontinue the religious practices prescribed by the Law. The regular Sabbath observances and the sacrifices at the altar were forbidden. So also were the gatherings of all the people for the three high ceremonies of the year. Altars of Zeus Olympius were erected and swine's flesh was offered upon them. To the pious Jews, this was appalling blasphemy. The possession of the scriptures was forbidden, the rolls were seized and burned.

Fired by mad ambition, Antiochus set out on the conquest of Egypt. This involved rivalry with Rome. In this plan Antiochus at first was successful, but when he seemed about to achieve his purpose Rome intervened and demanded his withdrawal from Egypt. The Roman official who brought this order drew a circle in the sand about Antiochus and told him to make up his mind before stepping outside the circle. Smarting from this humiliation and boiling with wrath, Antiochus started back to his own place. In his chagrin and bitterness, he was a dangerous person. On his way northward stood the city of Jerusalem where the uncompromising spirit of the Jews had shown itself in revolt. Upon the stubborn resisters of his imperial rule, Antiochus turned with all his seething wrath. The altars of the Temple were destroyed. A pagan altar with pagan practices was substituted. Swine's flesh was offered. Licentious rites were celebrated. The "continual," as the pious Jews called the daily morning and evening sacrifices, was stopped. These sacrifices symbolized for the people, day by day, the covenant proclaiming God's steadfast love which endures forever. The pious Jew called this desecration "the abomination of desolation," or "the abomination which makes desolate." This is a deeply emotional expression, full of the profound shock and sorrow of the saints.

In his madness Antiochus decreed the destruction of the Jewish scriptures. Death was the punishment of anyone found possessing one of these scrolls. The scrolls were systematically gathered, defaced, and burned. The persecuted had to hide in caves. But there they read or listened to the Law and the Prophets, and there they sang the Psalms. The wonder is that any copies survived this mad attempt to exterminate the Jewish scriptures. But these books proved their power in the face of the most destructive hatred ever used against them. They came through the fiery furnace more deeply cherished than ever before. They became Holy Scriptures with a new sense of their holiness.

3. THE BOOK OF DANIEL

The Book of Daniel is a unique part of the Old Testament and one of the most influential. In the Jewish canon, that which prevailed in the time of Jesus and the early church, the Book of Daniel is among the last books listed. See page 17. It is not included among the Prophets. It was a late book in the formation of the Old Testament. In the Christian arrangement, however, the Book of Daniel is placed fourth among the Prophets. But it is different from the books of prophecy in certain noticeable ways. It is an apocalypse (see page 123). It was the message which sustained the saints in the awful trials of the persecution under Antiochus. It is the sacred witness of the martyrs, a book of unique sanctity. During his persecuting madness, it was a fatal risk to say anything about Antiochus. But the saints could tell stories about Nebuchadnezzar, Belshazzar, and Darius, while having Antiochus in mind all the time. The underground always had to use secrecy and hidden symbols.

The Book of Daniel is the story of Daniel and his three friends, Shadrack, Meshach, and Abednego, in the courts of the Chaldeans and Persians. In these pagan situations, in the face of the commands of these tyrants, even when threatened by the burning, fiery furnace or the lion's den, these faithful servants of the Most High refused to be in any way disloyal to their God. "Daniel resolved that he would not defile himself" (Dan. 1:8). His friends, Shadrach, Meshach, and Abednego, answered the king, "Be it known to you, O King, that we will not serve your gods or worship the golden image which you have set up" (Dan. 3:18). That is the spirit which makes martyrs endure to the end. The Book of Daniel helped the Jews of the time of Antiochus Epiphanes (1) by holding before them an ideal character, (2) by telling them powerful stories (3) by giving them a strengthening interpretation of history, and (4) by assuring them of a resurrection. These points will be considered in turn.

(1) **Daniel, the ideal saint.** The saints are the consecrated men in whom is the Spirit of God. Daniel is the ideal saint in the setting of the rule of the tyrants. His three friends are also ideal saints. The Queen Mother, in Daniel 5:11, describes Daniel as "a man in whom is the spirit of the holy gods." Daniel was the product of the work of Ezra who "had set his heart to study the law of the Lord, and to do it, and to teach his statutes and ordinances in Israel" (Ezra 7:10). Under such a ruler as Nebuchadnezzar and under all the succession of the masters over Israel, it was not easy to follow Ezra in complete devotion to the Law. Daniel's resolution not to defile himself brought the

threat of death. For Shadrach, Meshach, and Abednego, their resolve not to bow down to the golden image resulted in their being cast into the burning, fiery furnace (Dan. 3:1-30). For Daniel, his persisting in his habits of prayer led to his being cast into the den of lions (Dan. 6:16). But these men were undaunted. The story of their heroism gave strength to the harried victims of Antiochus.

Upon the Jews in the days of Antiochus, death was decreed if they were found to have in their possession any part of the Old Testament, or if they refused to bow down to the image that Antiochus, the madman, had set up. They were tortured, refusing to accept release. They were mocked and scourged, even put in chains and imprisoned. "They were stoned, they were sawn in two, they were killed with the sword; they went about in skins of sheep and goats, destitute, afflicted, ill-treated—of whom the world was not worthy—wandering over deserts and mountains, and in dens and caves of the earth." See Hebrews 11:35-38. See also the stories of martyrdom in 2 Maccabees. Daniel and his friends became the ideals for such a people. The example of Daniel really worked. When the saints were told how Daniel dared the madness of Nebuchadnezzar, they dared the madness of Antiochus. In the same manner, Daniel continues to influence those who face temptation. The Book of Daniel is real creative literature in the hands of God. It functions by confronting God's people with an inspiring ideal.

(2) **The Book of Daniel strengthened the persecuted by matchless storytelling.** It not only presents an ideal character, but also presents him with supreme skill. The well-told story is one of the most effective means of reaching the mind and influencing the will. In the Book of Daniel are three of the best told and most widely known stories in all literature: The Fiery Furnace, The Lion's Den,

and The Handwriting upon the Wall. These have become a part of our literature. They possess enduring effectiveness. They owe their power in no small degree to the art of storytelling. When a man is telling a story because he is convinced that by his telling it deep decisions will be made and a true purpose will be enforced, he puts into the story the best that is in him. When a man of peculiarly rich gifts moved by the Spirit of God does this, then he pronounces the word of God, "living and active, sharper than any two-edged sword" (Heb. 4:12)—sharper than any sword of a tyrant.

(3) **The Book of Daniel helped the persecuted by giving them a strengthening interpretation of history.** In chapter 7, Daniel relates that in his vision he saw four great beasts and after them one like unto a son of man. That, in brief, is the interpretation of history. Kingdoms rise and fall, one after the other. They are all alike. They are like beasts. But in the end there will be one like a son of man, like man as created in the image of God, like man who is but little lower than God. This is the kingdom of the saints.

"And the kingdom and the dominion
    and the greatness of the kingdoms under the whole heaven
    shall be given to the people of the saints of the Most High;
their kingdom shall be an everlasting kingdom,
    and all dominions shall serve and obey them" (Dan. 7:28).

This philosophy of history is based on the purpose of God, on his purpose that there shall be a kingdom of saints instead of the kingdoms of bestial tyrants. When convinced of that purpose, the patience of the saints is established. Holding to this philosophy of history, God's people endured and came through victorious.

(4) **The Book of Daniel strengthened the persecuted by hope of a resurrection.** "But at that time your people

shall be delivered, every one whose name shall be found written in the book. And many of those who sleep in the dust of the earth shall awake, some to everlasting life, and some to shame and everlasting contempt" (Dan. 12:1-2). In the darkest hour of suffering, God brought this message of hope. He will straighten out the accounts. The saints who die for their faith, the martyrs, will enter into the everlasting kingdom which the Most High will establish. They may sleep in the dust of the earth, but they shall awake to everlasting life. Generally in the Old Testament there was no hope for life after death (Job 10:18-22; 14:7-12). As a result of this assurance in the Book of Daniel, belief in the resurrection became an article of faith among the pious Jews.

The Book of Daniel belongs to a special type of writings called apocalyptic. The other great example of this type is the last book of the New Testament, The Revelation (that is, the Apocalypse) of John. These two books are very much alike. There are a number of others which had popularity from about 200 B.C. to A.D. 200. They are rightly called "Tracts for Bad Times," for they all were written to the saints in days of persecution, such as were recurrent from the time of Antiochus into the reign of the Caesars. In these periods of acute danger, there was need of underground messages, secrets communicated in code, to avoid trouble with the authorities. In the underground, the message for the saints had to do two things at one and the same time: it had to reveal and it had to conceal; it must make something plain to the saints, but must say it in a way that the persecutors would not understand. The underground learns many ways of doing this. Such a writing was called an apocalypse or revelation, an unveiling. The words "mystery" and "reveal" are frequent in Daniel. The mystery is God's purpose. God reveals his purpose to the saints. Each chapter of Daniel is a revelation which was given to make the purpose of God known to his saints, but which was written in a dark and puzzling way to hide the message from the servants of the wicked king.

4. ACCEPTED AND UNACCEPTED BOOKS

In the days of the completion of the Old Testament, there were other Jewish writings which were on the margins of sanctity. These are called the Apocrypha, a word meaning hidden or concealed. This is not an accurate description of these works. "Noncanonical" is a better term. There are fourteen of these books: 1 Esdras ("Esdras" is a form of "Ezra"), 2 Esdras, Tobit, Judith, parts of Esther, The Wisdom of Solomon, Ecclesiasticus, Baruch, The Story of Susanna, The Song of the Three Holy Children (an addition to the Book of Daniel), The Story of Bel and the Dragon, The Prayer of Manasses, 1 Maccabees, and 2 Maccabees. Although these books were not included in the Hebrew Bible, they were included in the Greek translation and so passed into use in the Christian Church. The Roman Church accepts these books and prints them with the Old Testament. Because they were written from 150 B.C. on, they help us understand many things in Jewish thinking and history. First Maccabees is a fine piece of historical writing. It relates the story of the persecution by Antiochus IV, the revolt by the Maccabees, and the establishment of the Maccabean kingdom. It might well have been included among the Old Testament books of history. It would fit in admirably after Nehemiah.

Then there were the books which did not get into even the Apocrypha. In Jude, verse 14, reference is made to Enoch and he is quoted as a prophet. A collection of writings under the name of Enoch has been discovered, and it has proven very important in understanding this period. So have a considerable number of other books found in the old monasteries of the East. They have helped modern scholars greatly and show how active in a literary way this period was.

The formation of the Old Testament took place in a period when these other Jewish writings were current. When the books of the Old Testament are compared with these other writings, there is a strong feeling of the guidance of God in the formation of the Old Testament. Conviction as to the inspiration of the Old Testament is strengthened. The providence of God in the work of the canonization of the Law, Prophets, and Writings is evident. With this collection the chosen people were prepared to be a peculiar people amid the tensions of the Greek world, both to withstand their persecutors and to be a light to the nations. God blessed his people and made them a blessing according to his own good will in the completion of the Old Testament.

Thus, the Old Testament was completed and entered into the life of the world as a functioning power. It is not a library. It is not a collection of ancient documents. The Old Testament is the Word of God, and it possesses its own inherent strength. It is God's unfolding revelation of himself at work during the long generations of history in a people chosen by himself to be blessed and to be a blessing to all the families of the earth.

10

THE PRAISES OF ISRAEL

OF ALL THE OLD TESTAMENT BOOKS, The Psalms is most cherished by Bible readers. Some of the best known and most frequently used Bible passages are found in this collection of hymns and prayers. The vibrant, praiseful, religious life of Israel in its many moods came to beautiful expression in these ever-living songs.

Worship is the very heart of religion. Law and Prophets must be accompanied by prayer and song. In The Psalms, the worshiper enters into the whole range of religious feelings, its dark moments of despair and its glad moments of hope, its valleys of doubt and its mountains of certainty. The Old Testament is of unfailing value because it is full of prayer and because the prayers are so varied and so beautifully expressed.

The God of Israel awakened this spirit of worship. By his gracious acts of salvation and by his steadfast covenant-love, he stirred his people to sing. Enthusiasm is characteristic of the worship of Israel. The psalms become a Hallelujah chorus. "Praise the Lord" is a shout of gladness. The reader must join in these prayers and songs, if he would understand and interpret the Old Testament.

1. THE PLACE OF WORSHIP IN ISRAEL

The altar was at the center of the life of Israel. Everywhere, always, there was the altar where God and his people met. Wherever Abraham journeyed he set up an altar and worshiped his God. This was only the pile of field stones of the nomad's camp, but Abraham advanced from place to place with his flocks in humble awareness of the presence of God. Jacob took a stone and called it Beth-el, House of God. Moses led the people to the Mountain of God to gather the people about an altar for the making of the covenant. As the Israelites entered Canaan and settled in the village life, they built their local altars. Gideon tore down the altar of baal in his village and built an altar to the God of Israel. These were all simple piles of field stones where the people of a village carried on their simple ceremonies with prayers and songs. In time Shiloh became the most prominent place of worship, because the ark of the Lord was there. A temple of some kind, with a regular resident priesthood of the family of Eli, furnished a special altar to which different tribes could come annually.

When David had fully established the kingdom with the newly captured Jerusalem as its capital, he began plans for a temple and a royal residence. Solomon completed this work. Then there was a building more glorious than any other in the whole of Israel, a marvelous new temple. It was a royal sanctuary connected with the other royal buildings and under the control of the king. Its altar was a great construction of hewn stone arranged for elaborate sacrificial rituals.

The people in general continued to worship at the simple altars where their fathers had met with their God generation after generation. When Jeroboam revolted against the tyranny of Solomon, two temples were built, one at Bethel in the southern part of Jeroboam's kingdom and one at Dan in the north. So for a long time there were many local altars, a royal sanctuary at Dan with its priesthood, another at Bethel with its priesthood, another at

Jerusalem with its priesthood of the house of Zadok. King Josiah attempted to centralize all the worship in Jerusalem. But naturally the people preferred their own altars. Josiah's reformation did not last long and the old ways prevailed. The local places, however, were always in danger of the corrupting baal practices. The "high places" became debasing because of the fertility rites. What Israel needed was one place for the worship of the One God of Israel.

The Temple in Jerusalem with its altar was destroyed by Nebuchadnezzar. Israel was left without an altar and without a central place of worship. To pious Israel, that was the deepest woe of the Exile. There was no holy setting for the holy practices of worship. The outward arrangements for the ceremonies were gone and the name of their God was being profaned. The Temple of Solomon in Jerusalem had been built upon a rock, an outcropping ledge at the top of the holy hill. That remained. To this sacred site pilgrims sometimes came during the desolation. Finally Cyrus issued the decree which authorized the rebuilding of the Temple. The returning exiles at once rebuilt the altar. Proper worship could then be resumed. Only after a number of years of hard times was the Temple rebuilt under the revivalistic urging of Haggai and Zechariah.

The Second Temple was not so glorious as that built by Solomon, but it was adequate for the small nation in and about Jerusalem. Now, at last, there was one altar, one holy place, for the worship of the One God by all the people. At the time of the persecution by Antiochus Epiphanes this altar was destroyed and another was erected to Zeus on which swine were sacrificed. This was the "abomination of desolation." But under the Maccabees the altar was reconstructed, an event still celebrated by the Jews. Herod the Great rebuilt the Temple and its altar in greater glory than it had ever known. But in A.D. 70 all was utterly destroyed, never to rise again. So the history of the chosen people can be sketched in the history of the altar.

The Temple was a building for the ceremonies connected with the sacrificial offerings. It stood in the midst of a walled-off area arranged in several courts, each one more holy than the preceding one. Steps led up to the Temple with its holy place and the holy of holies. The people entered the lower court, the priests the next, the high priests the third. Elaborate ceremonies were carried on by the priests who were carefully trained for every movement. The Levites were organized into choirs. The psalms were used in this setting. They gave meaning and beauty to the ceremonies. By means of the psalms, the ritual was made into deeper worship. The psalms furnished prayers and songs which the people could learn and could carry home for the enrichment of their lives.

The psalms were used later in the synagogues which arose as the local places of weekly worship. Instead of the old altars at the high places, there grew up these houses of instruction in the Law. They were also places of prayer and praise. The psalms became the Hymnal and Prayer Book of the people. They furnished for the daily life the language by which God approached his people and his people worshiped him as their Creator and Savior. From the synagogue the psalms entered the church.

2. HEBREW POETRY

The psalms are poetry. A great deal of the Old Testament is poetry, especially the prophetical books. Until recently, our manner of printing the Bible had concealed the poetical form of many of the writings, yet their rhythms catch the attention of any thoughtful reader. Hebrew poetry does not employ the rhyming of the ends of lines. Instead, it uses a balancing of lines which is called parallelism.

"The earth is the Lord's and the fulness thereof,
    the world and those who dwell therein;
for he has founded it upon the seas,
    and established it upon the rivers" (Ps. 24:1-2).

The second line in each of these couplets parallels the
first line; it reinforces it by repeating the thought in a
different way. Psalm 19:1-4 shows this in words with which
we are familiar. In psalm after psalm, this is evident. Then
there are variations by the use of three and four lines.
Parallelism is a simple device which furnishes numerous
modes of expression for the wide range of feeling awakened
by the sense of God's living presence.

3. PSALMS OF PRAISE

Our word "psalm" comes from the Greek word *psalmos*
which was used in reference to playing on musical instruments. "Psaltery" is the name of a stringed instrument.
"Psalter" is the name for the whole book of psalms. It
has been said that a psalm needs a singer and musical accompaniment. Many instruments are mentioned: trumpet,
lute, harp, timbrel, strings, pipes, cymbals (see Ps. 150).
Reference to the accompanying music occur in the headings
of many psalms. We do not know the meaning of most
of the terms. "To the chief musician" appears frequently,
but translators are uncertain about the term. Names of
tunes are given but the tunes themselves have not been
handed down. "Selah" has lost its meaning for us. But
all these terms indicate that the psalms are songs, and that
music was an important feature of their use. They are
largely hymns for worship in Temple and synagogue. The
Hebrew heading of this book is "Book of Praises."

As the Book of Praises, the Psalter contains many invocations by which the worshipers call upon God and
glorify his name, many stirring summonses to the people

to come and praise God, many doxologies in which the praise is concluded. That is, the psalms furnish the fitting ways in which to approach God, to praise him, and to bless his holy name. Here are some examples.

An Invocation:

"Lord, thou has been our dwelling place
    in all generations.
Before the mountains were brought forth,
    or ever thou hadst formed the earth and the world,
        from everlasting to everlasting thou art God" (Ps. 90:1-2).

A Call to Worship:

"O come, let us sing to the Lord;
    let us make a joyful noise to the rock of our salvation"
                            (Ps. 95:1).

A Benediction:

"Blessed be the Lord, the God of Israel,
    from everlasting to everlasting!
    Amen and Amen" (Ps. 41:13).

When reading through the Psalter, one comes upon these invocations, calls to worship, and doxologies time after time. The Psalter has given to all worshipers these essential means of praise.

Psalm 8 is one of the greatest gifts of the Old Testament. This short song is pure praise. There is no request for any favor, no petition for help, no problem.

"O Lord, our Lord,
    how majestic is thy name in all the earth."

So the psalm begins and so it ends. It celebrates God's mindfulness of man and the dignity and worth of man, who was created but little lower than God and given dominion over the works of God's hands. But all is a hymn of praise, of enthusiastic praise—a glorifying of God's excellence. Psalm 8 is the truest expression of this spirit which is characteristic of the psalms.

Psalm 24 is of different form, but it, too, is vibrant with praise. It is a song for the worshipers as they come to the Temple. First, it celebrates the glory of God (vss. 1-2). Next it tells the conditions for coming to worship (vss. 3-6). Then the song of the worshiper is given (vss. 7-10). Psalm 24 is a rousing antiphonal hymn which should have full instrumental accompaniment. Here is praise which must be shouted by a full chorus. Listen to the question asked by some deep-voiced priest, "Who is the King of glory?" Then hear the whole congregation's full vocal response, together with trumpet and cymbals. Such praise must be repeated and it is repeated.

Psalm 148 is full of praise. It begins, "Praise the Lord!" It ends, "Praise the Lord!" Line after line calls "Praise the Lord." This is one of the hallelujah psalms. "Hallel" is the verb "to praise." *Hallelu* is the imperative of this verb. *Iah, Jah,* or *Jah* is the short form of Yahweh which is used in compounds. Hallelujah, therefore, is a strong summons to praise Yahweh the Lord. The Psalter has given us this unique word. There are in the Psalter groups of psalms called the Hallels. (See Pss. 105-107; 111-118; 146-150.) These are vigorous Songs of Praise. Psalm 150 is the most exultant Hallel of all. It should be read with ascending force, with orchestral accompaniment, with a climaxing Hallelujah which can be heard afar off. Such was the enthusiasm awakened by the God of Deliverance and Salvation. This stirring praise survived even the days when Israel tasted its deepest woe and chanted mournful lamentations.

"O sing to the Lord a new song,
   for he has done marvelous things!

*   *   *   *   *

He has remembered his steadfast love and faithfulness
   to the house of Israel" (Ps. 98:1-3).

They sang such psalms as they came out of captivity. They
continued to sing praises all their days.

4. DIDACTIC PSALMS

Many psalms were composed for the purpose of instruc
tion. Teachers (scribes) wrote psalms to help their pupils
in memorization. Such psalms were written in very formal
patterns. Psalm 119 is the longest and most formally constructed of the didactic psalms. It is what is called an
acrostic or alphabetical poem. There are twenty-two sections in accordance with the twenty two letters of the Hebrew alphabet. Each section is made up of eight verses of
two lines each, and the first line of each of the eight verses
in a section begins with the letter of the alphabet for that
section. The first section, for example, uses the first letter
of the Hebrew alphabet, "aleph," and each of the eight
verses begins with a word whose first letter is "aleph."
Throughout the one hundred and seventy-six verses of this
psalm, this very formal structure is maintained with mechanical exactitude. Although it produced a form which is
artificial, it gave a scheme for memorization. The amazing
thing is the spirit of sincere devotion and praise maintained within this formal regimentation. How deep the
piety of the devoted scribe who could fill this artificial structure with such unwavering strength of feeling!

This acrostic or alphabetical design is found also in
Psalms 9, 25, 34, 37, 111, 112, and 145. This method of
writing is familiar in many children's rhymes. A is for_____,
B is for _____, etc. It is difficult to reproduce this in an Eng-
lish translation. The Smith-Goodspeed version is helpful.
The American Standard Version and the Westminster Study
Edition indicate the alphabetical sections of Psalm 119.

After Ezra bound the people to the study and observance of the Law, schools were needed and good materials for memorization. Pupils were without books of their own. They had to learn the Word by systematic memorization. The alphabetical psalms met this need. Although so mechanical in its structure, Psalm 119 contains passages of superior worth which show the true spirit of the writer and the spirit he aimed to cultivate in the pupils.

> "Open my eyes, that I may behold
>   wondrous things out of thy law" (Ps. 119:18).

> "Oh, how I love thy law!
>   It is my meditation all the day" (Ps. 119:97).

> "Thy word is a lamp to my feet
>   and a light to my path" (Ps. 119:105).

These verses and others like them witness the deep, living piety of the psalmist. With Psalm 119, compare Psalm 1, another such didactic poem. How valuable it has been in the teaching work of the church!

5. PSALMS OF THE INNER LIFE

In The Psalms, God is known as the searching Presence in the inner life. "The word of God is living and active"— and "piercing" (Heb. 4:12). This piercing power of the Word is seen in certain of the profoundest psalms. "Deep calls unto deep" as God searches the soul. This is true particularly in Psalm 139, which might be headed, "The Ever-present, Searching Presence of God." The awareness of God to the psalmist is wonderful (v. 6), precious (v. 17), and beyond estimation (v. 18). The psalm is to be read with this consciousness of the living, active, piercing Presence as life's most blessed experience. The psalm is a prayer.

This prayer begins with a joyful confession, "O Lord, thou hast searched me and known me!" It concludes with an earnest request, "Search me, O God, and know my heart!" All of the psalm stands bracketed between these two petitions. In verses 2-6 the psalmist acknowledges God as present in the whole inner life and as knowing the thoughts and intentions of the heart. In verses 7-12 he acknowledges God as present wherever one may go. In verses 12-16 he speaks with awe of God's presence and of his creative work in the prenatal processes of life. In verses 17-18 the psalmist pauses to celebrate gratefully the preciousness and wonder of the presence of God in his inner life, wherever he may be. Then comes a fervent prayer for separation from sinners who do not recognize and accept God's presence. Finally, the climax is a petition to God to search him and lead him in that way of life which never fails.

There is nothing deeper or truer than Psalm 139. The psalmist knew God directly, personally, intimately. He was aware of God in the very processes of his thinking. This psalm must be placed along with the Law and the Prophets as part of God's revelation of the inner reality of his relationship with man.

Psalm 51 is another record of the deep, searching presence of God in the inner life. In this respect it closely resembles Psalm 139.

> "Behold, thou desirest truth in the inward being;
>   therefore teach me wisdom in my secret heart.
>   *   *   *   *   *
> Create in me a clean heart, O God,
>   and put a new and right spirit within me.
>   *   *   *   *   *
> The sacrifice acceptable to God is a broken spirit;
>   a broken and contrite heart, O God, thou wilt not despise"
>   (Ps. 51:6, 10, 17).

No psalm gives clearer evidence of God's present, piercing, searching of the inner life of thought and feeling, of attitudes and affections. This is a psalm which is indispensable for right relations with God. Psalm 51 begins in the spirit of true approach to God, with an acknowledgment of the mercy of God, his steadfast love, and his abundant mercy. The worshiper comes before God with the true petition: blot out, wash, cleanse. He makes the true confession: my iniquity, my transgression, my sin.

Throughout The Psalms there is this clear awareness of the activity of God doing what needs to be done in creating a new heart. The psalmist senses God at work in washing thoroughly, in cleansing, purging, and recreating the inner being. The national worship of Israel was at the altar with its elaborate, regulated ceremony of offerings, especially the sacrifice of animals. The outward rites of this system could be performed with no direct personal sense of the presence of God, and the offerings could be made as a means of purchasing the favor of God with no personal change of life. The prophets had to rebuke with all the force of their preaching the sin of seeking to purchase escape from the consequences of sin by means of this sacrificial system. (See Amos 4:4-5; 5:21-24; Hos. 6:6; Isa. 1: 10-17; Jer. 7:5-7; Ps. 40:6-8; Deut. 10:12-13; and especially Micah 6:6-8. Compare Matt. 9:13; 12:7; 22:37.) Psalm 51 is the true revelation of right relations with God.

The forgiveness of God deals with iniquity, transgression, sin. "Against thee, thee only have I sinned" (Ps. 51:4). Sin is a term which is relevant to our personal relations with God. If there is no God, there is no sin; although there may be misdemeanors and crimes in relations of persons in the civil order, wrongs which can be handled by courts. But the charge of sin does not apply in any court. Sin is not recognized except where the Moral Ruler of the universe is recognized. The Old Testament has a good deal to say about sin, because there is such a profound awareness of God as the Holy One, the Lord of Heaven and earth, whose rule is righteousness and justice. A wrong deed is a crime against man, but it is also a sin against God. This profound moral sense produced the deep searching of heart which this psalmist expresses. Psalm 51 gives the clearest recognition of the inner nature of sin, and it shows also the glad, joyful awareness of God in his recreating of the heart. No other psalm has helped in the inward spiritual realities of sin and forgiveness as has Psalm 51.

6. PSALMS OF THE TROUBLED MIND

"Out of the depths I cry to thee, O Lord!" (Ps. 130:1). The psalms bear evidence of all the woes which Israel endured, the sorrows of individuals as well as the afflictions of the nations, sufferings which were produced by foes without and by evil within. The afflicted have always found understanding and comfort in the psalms, for there is no depth from which men cry but what that depth and that cry were known in Israel.

> "Is it nothing to you, all you who pass by?
>   Look and see
> if there is any sorrow like my sorrow
>   which was brought upon me,
> which the Lord inflicted
>   on the day of his fierce anger" (Lam. 1:12).

The problem of suffering, especially the suffering of the innocent, is a perplexity which arises time after time in the Old Testament. Many psalms show the anguish of this question and the way in which the suffering was endured.

Psalm 73 is a revelation of God at work in such a troubled mind. In vs. 1 the fundamental assurance of the psalmist is stated:

"Truly God is good to the upright,
    to those who are pure in heart."

Or, as the King James Version renders it, "Surely God is good to Israel, even to such as are pure in heart." The psalmist had been taught this truth and accepted it. But how did this square with the facts of life as he experienced them? The equation of life should be: "Piety brings Prosperity; Impiety brings Adversity." In the life of this psalmist it had not worked that way. His piety had been followed by adversity, while the impiety of others had resulted in prosperity. This was a severe problem.

The psalmist in his confession leads us through his experience as he faced this contradiction.

"But as for me, my feet had almost stumbled,
    my steps had well nigh slipped.
For I was envious of the arrogant,
    when I saw the prosperity of the wicked."
            *   *   *   *   *
"All in vain have I kept my heart clean
    and washed my hands in innocence.
For all the day long I have been stricken,
    and chastened every morning" (Ps. 73:2-3, 13-14).

This troubled soul saw that while he sought after good, the wicked were taking possession of the goods. Envy, that deep danger of the soul, sprang up in his mind. He began drifting into that skepticism which says, "How can God know?" Vss. 2-14 tell how he was slipping.

But God checked him when he was about to stumble. This is related in vss. 15-20. The psalmist was made to think, to think painfully, for hard thinking is the way of escape from the folly of the world. God made him consider the effect of skeptical talk. God led him to the place of worship to do his thinking. There, in the words of the Law and the Prophets, he considered the final outcome of the wicked. So he was checked in the slippery way. In vss. 21-22 he confesses that his envy of the wicked was really thinking like the beast who wants only his fill. Then comes the light, the answer to his problem in vss. 23-26. God himself is the highest good.

> "Whom have I in heaven but thee?
>   And there is nothing upon earth that I desire beside thee"
>   (Ps. 73:26).

There is in Psalm 73 no philosophic solution of the problem of suffering, but there is in the midst of suffering the discovery that God himself is present—"the strength of my heart and my portion forever." The psalm closes with an act of consecration.

> "But for me it is good to be near God;
>   · I have made the Lord God my refuge,
>   that I may tell of all thy works" (Ps. 73:28).

Psalm 73 carries us step by step through a very real experience of painful thinking. It leads us along the right path when we must struggle against being envious of the prosperity of evil men. It guides us into the one good of life, our personal relationship with God. Compare Psalms 37, 49, and 94, which deal with this same problem. Note also Psalms 42 and 43, which are really one psalm.

> "Why are you cast down, O my soul,
>   and why are you disquieted within me?
>   Hope in God; for I shall again praise him?
>   my help and my God" (Pss. 42:5, 11; 43:5).

The psalms have much to help the troubled mind, for many of them came out of troubled minds.

7. THE STRUCTURE OF THE PSALTER

Looking at the Book of Psalms as a whole, one hundred and fifty are numbered. There is some duplication. See Psalms 14 and 53. Psalms 42 and 43, as stated above, are really one. Psalm 19 seems to be a combination of two. The book as a whole is a collection of collections. See Psalm 72:20: "The prayers of David, the son of Jesse, are ended." This reads like the close of a collection of Davidic Psalms. The following collections (not including every psalm) appear to have been brought together thus: (1) The First Davidic Psalter, Psalms 3-41; (2) The Second Davidic Psalter, Psalms 51-72; (3) The Third Davidic Psalter, Psalms 139-145; (4) The Korah Psalter, Psalms 42-49, 84-85, 87-88; (5) The Asaph Psalter, Psalms 50, 73-83; (6) The Hallelujah Psalter, Psalms 105-107, 111-118, 146-150; (7) The Pilgrim Psalter, Psalms 120-134. The Praises of Israel were very much alive. They grew through the centuries as the experience of the living God deepened.

8. THE AUTHORS OF THE PSALMS

The most common name at the heading of the psalms is that of David. Moses' name appears for Psalm 90, Solomon's for Psalm 72. Psalm 88 is ascribed to Heman the Ezrahite and Psalm 89 to Ethan the Ezrahite. Then there are the psalms of Korah and of Asaph. Several psalms without names were called "orphans" by the rabbis. Psalm 102 has an interesting note, "A prayer of one afflicted, when he is faint and pours out his complaint before the Lord." But David is the fountainhead of the psalmists. Just as Moses is the great name in the Law, so David is the great name in The Psalms. He was a poet and singer. He planned for the building of the Temple and is credited with the beginnings of the Temple choirs. The expression at the head of the Davidic psalms is "To David," which may indicate either authorship or honorific dedication.

9. THE ENDURING POWER OF THE PSALMS

The psalms appear in the church service regularly. Is there ever an hour of church worship without the use of something from the psalms? How many invocations, calls to worship, responsive readings, responses, and doxologies are taken from the psalms! Our Christian hymnody is based on the psalms. They are indispensable in Christian devotion. What writing is better known than the Twenty-third Psalm? This has become the universal song of God's people. It is the supreme evidence of the inward genuineness and vitality of the praises of Israel.

11

THE WISDOM OF ISRAEL

WISDOM, UNDERSTANDING, INSTRUCTION, AND DISCI-
PLINE are important words in the vocabulary of the Old
Testament. This book of God's revelations of himself contains Law, Prophets, Psalms, and Wisdom. For her instructions, Israel had priests, prophets, and sages. The wisdom
of the sages is found from the beginning. As the discipline
of the nation went on through all the people had to undergo
and undertake, wisdom became more and more prized.
These sages gathered the wise sayings of everyday life, feeling that in these proverbs God was instructing the people.
They studied life in an effort to understand it more deeply.
They sought to put their wisdom into effective form for
teaching. Finally, they put the accumulated riches of their
searching into books. These books are included in the last
division of the Old Testament.

Beginning with Ezra, the scribes became of great importance in the life of the nation. As teachers the scribes were
concerned with wisdom, and good scribes became sages
whose words of wisdom were treasured by their pupils and
handed on from generation to generation. As the Greeks
entered into the life of the Jews and began to influence
them through their philosophy, the pursuit of wisdom as
philosophic thought was stimulated and new books of wisdom were produced. The work of the sages was a long,
ever-increasing stream.

142

1. THE BEGINNING OF WISDOM

"The fear of the Lord is the beginning of wisdom" (Prov. 9:10). This familiar saying is the proper starting point for considering that group of books in the Old Testament known as the Wisdom Literature. The group consists of Job, Proverbs, and Ecclesiastes, with which certain psalms might be included, such as Psalm 1; 19:7-14; and 119. In later writings, this type is found in Ecclesiasticus, the Wisdom of Solomon, *Pirke Aboth* (Sayings of the Fathers), and the Epistle of James. "Fear," in such sayings as Proverbs 1:7 and 9:10 does not denote being frightened by God. It means awe, reverence, humility, the proper attitude of the creature before his Creator. This fear may have its moments of dread, but the constant attitude is reverence for the Holy One. It is that attitude which man has when he kneels before the Creator and Lord of the universe in reverential obedience.

For Israel this fear was that which had been awakened by God as known in Israel, by his choosing them as his people, delivering them, making the covenant with them, and keeping covenant with them in steadfast love. Such fear had been taught by the prophets. Isaiah's experience in the Temple is one of the clearest moments of such fear of the Lord (Isa. 6:1-13). In his vision, Isaiah saw the Lord sitting upon a throne high and lifted up, and he heard the seraphim in their antiphonal praise singing,

"Holy, holy, holy is the Lord of hosts;
the whole earth is full of his glory."

This profound awareness of the presence and glory of God is the fear of the Lord. The pious Israelite expressed it in his study of the Law and in his praises and prayers in The Psalms.

This fear was for God as he made himself known in the life of the nation. The people had found that their God was the God of loving-kindness, steadfast love, justice, righteousness, and holiness. So he was worthy to be worshiped with all one's heart, with all one's soul, with all one's might. The *Shema* expresses this fear of the Lord (Deut. 6:6-9). The Ten Commandments summon God's people to reverential awe and obedience (Ex. 20:1-17). The Lamentations wrung from the heart of the Exiles by their sense of guilt and shame expresses the fear of the Lord in deep dread of his judgment. Such songs of joy as Psalms 95-100 are overflowing with that grateful acknowledgment of the goodness of God which is the fear of the Lord, for it is the awe of amazement. Fear runs the whole gamut of man's moods, but its constant attitude is awe, reverential awe.

Wisdom is in God and comes from God. Man learns wisdom only through knowing God. Folly consists in not recognizing God or fearing him. Two statements about the fool warn those who would find wisdom: "The fool says in his heart 'There is no God'" (Ps. 14:1); and "Fools despise wisdom and instruction" (Prov. 1:7). Wisdom is recognizing God as present in and at work in everyday life, as the moral ruler and instructor. The wisdom of Israel, that is, the wisdom peculiar to Israel, has as its unique truth the knowledge and instruction of God as he was made known through the prophets.

Wise sayings are found among all people. At the level of prudence and practicality these sayings may be much the same. In Egypt a document has been discovered containing the proverbs of Amen-em-ope, a sage who lived about 900 B.C., i.e., near the time of Solomon. His wise sayings and those of Proverbs 22:17—24:22 are closely related. As keen observations about life, they are equal in value with the Proverbs. The wisdom of Israel, however, is spoken always in reverent awareness of Yahweh, the unique God of Israel. Just as the Ten Commandments begin with God's declaration, "I am the Lord your God, who brought you out of the land of Egypt, out of the house of bondage," so also every saying of the Hebrew men of wisdom is made in the light of God's gracious act of redemption. Together with the words of instruction spoken by these sages, let the *Shema* (Deut. 6:5) be repeated. Then the practical advice will have deeper meaning. The words of the prophets, the songs of the psalmists, and the services at the Temple altar—all should have as their accompaniment the advice and exhortations of the sages. The true pupils of the books of wisdom were always worshipers, grateful, whole-hearted worshipers of their Creator and Redeemer. To such the fear of the Lord is indeed the beginning of wisdom.

2. THE PROVERBS

This book has so many sections and so many separate sayings that it is not well constructed for continuous reading from beginning to end. It should be taken in regulated doses of varying length. Brief, practical comments on life and sayings in praise of wisdom make up the contents. The Book of Proverbs is a collection of collections, and accumulation of the riches of the ages. This is indicated by various headings. For example: "These also are proverbs of Solomon which the men of Hezekiah king of Judah copied" (Prov. 25:1); and "Have I not written for you thirty sayings of admonition and knowledge?" (Prov. 22:20).

The divisions of Proverbs are as follows: (1) The Praises of Wisdom, Proverbs of Solomon (Prov. 1-9). (2) Proverbs for the Practical Guidance of Life, Proverbs of Solomon (Prov. 10:1—22:16). (3) The Words of the Wise,

(Prov. 22:17—24:22). (4) Proverbs for Practical Guidance, Proverbs of Solomon (Prov. 25:1—29:27). (5) The Words of Agur (Prov. 30:1-23). (6) The Words of Lemuel; the Advice of the Queen Mother to her Son (Prov. 31:1-9). (7) The Ideal Wife (Prov. 31:10-31). These sections indicate the processes of accumulation as God, through a long period, worked in many minds—in the mind of the common man observing the facts of his life and in the mind of the sage meditating upon wisdom, in the farmer's observations and in the king's pronouncements.

In such a section as Proverbs 10:1—22:16, brief, pithy observations of daily life are found generally in two-line parallelism. These sayings are homely, witty, salty, practical, prudential. Often they are the guide to good housekeeping, better farming, or more profitable business. In them the reader enters the homes, shops, and fields of the common man and hears the voice of experience. So also he can enter the palaces of kings and nobles and hear their observations on folly and wisdom.

In such a section as Proverbs 1-9, there is a sustained discussion of wisdom. Here the sage is a philosopher. Proverbs 8:22-31 is especially interesting for wisdom is personalized. "The Lord created me [Wisdom] at the beginning of his work, for the first of his acts of old." This statement reminds one of the opening declaration of the Gospel of John, "In the beginning was the Word." The philosophic sage is seaching the very nature of God. This philosophic section stands in interesting contrast to the earthiness of many proverbs.

Wisdom is a characteristic belonging to God and a gift which God bestows upon man. The term covers the whole range of the understanding of life, from human common sense condensed into maxims which fix themselves in memory to the divine word finding expression in a profound philosophy of life. The wise man is one who lives in the midst of the affairs of life, while maintaining a sense of God's penetrating wisdom throughout the whole of that life.

3. THE BOOK OF JOB

This book is recognized as one of the supreme classics in the whole range of literature. It is one of the profoundest of all writings. Job comes within the classification of Wisdom Literature. Surely its author was one of the sagest of sages. But Job is a unique book. There is none other like it in the Bible or elsewhere. God used an exceptional genius in this exceptional dramatic writing. It is rightly called "the Drama of Job." Its theme is the problem of the suffering of the innocent. This theme perplexes the mind of man, for it raises a question concerning the righteousness of God. This is a persistent theme through the Old Testament, for the Old Testament, as a whole, tells the story of a people who suffered many tragedies.

A case is presented: Job, a man who "was blameless and upright, one who feared God and who turned away from evil" (Job 1:1). That verse should be underscored. It is the proposition of the book. It is emphasized by repetition in Job 1:8 and 2:3: "Have you considered my servant Job, that there is none like him on earth, a blameless and upright man, who fears God and turns away from evil?" This is the case presented in this drama. Job must be seen through the whole dialogue as God describes him, a righteous, innocent man.

Job is a prosperous man, prosperous beyond others in property and family. Then comes sudden, unexplained, undeserved affliction in fullest measure. Job suffers the loss of his property, his family, and his health. In this way the problem was thrust upon him. The Book of Job, in dramatic dialogue, pictures Job in his agony of mind in this extreme affliction. Israel's problem of suffering is concentrated in this most acute case. Why does an innocent and really pious man who obeys God's commandments suffer? The problem is the more agonizing because it brings the justice of God into question. Habakkuk had cried out against this seeming injustice when the Chaldeans ruthlessly afflicted the world:

> "Thou who are of purer eyes than to behold evil
>   and canst not look on wrong,
> why dost thou look on faithless men,
>   and art silent when the wicked swallows up
>   the man more righteous than he?" (Hab. 1:13).

Why do the righteous suffer? Why does God allow the suffering of the righteous?

The case in the Book of Job, then, is the case of an innocent man, that is, one who does not merit the loss of property, family, and health. The book is a protracted discussion of that question by means of penetrating dialogue. The scene of the argument is upon a pile of ashes, with Job scraping the sores which afflict him from head to foot. The other parties in the dialogue are three friends who have come from afar to mourn with Job—Eliphaz, Bildad, and Zophar. Later there is a young fellow named Elihu. These friends want to help Job, but they do not. In fact they prove "miserable comforters" who only increase his agony. In the conclusion, the Lord condemns them: "After the Lord had spoken these words to Job, the Lord said to Eliphaz the Temanite: 'My wrath is kindled against you and against your two friends; for you have not spoken of me what is right, as my servant Job has'" (Job 42:7). This repudiation of the three friends must be kept in mind when reading the dialogue. These friends argue with Job in speech after speech in which they claim that they are declaring the truth of God, but in the end God says that they have not spoken what is right, as Job has. So the words of these friends should not be quoted as the word of God.

Another fact must be kept in mind. The debate is in the setting of a strong belief in the law of retribution. Piety brings prosperity: impiety brings adversity; prosperity proves piety: adversity proves impiety. That is a simple formula of life. Now, according to that law, the adversity of Job was a clear indication of his impiety. The only answer that the friends had for Job was that he had sinned and should repent. All their speeches kept pounding away on that theory. They state the law of retribution with eloquence, logic, vehemence, and finally with ill temper. But Job holds fast to his integrity. He will not speak what is not true regarding himself and he will not curse God.

In all this debate, Job is in the deepest distress and perplexity of mind. He is tossed to and fro by the tension of hope and despair. At times his thoughts sink into skepticism. At other times he rises into the certainties of faith. He speaks sometimes rashly and sometimes rationally. In irritation he cries out sharply against his would-be comforters. In the belief of his day there was no clear and reassuring teaching regarding the future life. It seemed that death was the same for all, for man and beast, and that they who went down into the pit could not praise God (Ps. 30:9; Job 10:18-22; 14:7-12). But Job reaches out toward a future life when the wrongs of this life will be righted and he will know God directly. His hope verges on a comforting belief in the future, but he does not arrive at any enduring assurance. The words of Job are the painful thinking of a storm-tossed soul. He is sick in body and in mind. His friends were bound in their doctrine and never could come to a sympathetic understanding of suffering.

After the three friends have spoken in the three rounds of the dialogue and have said all that they could, and after their tempers have moved them to words they ought never to have uttered, a young fellow by the name of Elihu steps forward in the self-confidence of inexperience and verbalizes at length in several rounds of oratorical boxing. His adolescent condescension toward old age and his repetitions of what has already been said do not help Job in his deep perplexity (Job 32-37).

Then the Lord answered Job out of the whirlwind (Job 38-42). This is one of the most remarkable parts of this unique book. God seems to bear down upon Job with the overwhelming power of a mighty storm. It is the Creator who speaks to the creature to awaken in him that fear of the Lord which is the beginning of wisdom. Job needed to bow in humble reverence before the All-Sufficient One who knows and understands all. God does not give any explanation of Job's problem. Instead, he stands before Job as the Lord Almighty. Job must leave his case with God, the All-Sufficient. This helps where the arguments of his friends had been of no avail. Job's response is the answer of one who for himself has freshly discovered God and who humbly rests in that assuring presence. When he speaks, it is to say:

"I know that thou canst do all things,
    and that no purpose of thine can be thwarted.
'Who is this that hides counsel without knowledge?'
Therefore I have uttered what I did not understand,
    things too wonderful for me, which I did not know.
'Hear, and I will speak;
    I will question you, and you declare to me.'
I had heard of thee by the hearing of the ear,
    but now my eye sees thee;
therefore I despise myself,
    and repent in dust and ashes" (Job 42:2-6).

Job did not discover a formal answer to his problems, but he discovered God. "Now my eye sees thee." That is the glorious answer. This conclusion recalls Psalm 73, which tells of another's struggle with this perplexing problem of suffering. The psalmist found what Job did:

> "Nevertheless I am continually with thee;
> thou dost hold my right hand. . . .
> "Whom have I in heaven but thee?
> And there is nothing upon earth that I desire besides thee"
> (Ps. 73:23, 25).

The Book of Job gives us one insight into suffering which Job himself did not possess. This drama is set on two stages, on earth and in heaven. We have the earthly scene, in which we learn of Job's piety and prosperity (Job 1:1-5); the heavenly scene, with Satan's challenge, "Does Job serve God for naught?" and God's confidence in Job (Job 1:6-12); and again the earthly scene, with Job's loss of property and family. In all this, Job did not sin or charge God with wrong (Job 1:13-22). Job 2:1-6 brings again the heavenly scene, and we hear Satan's second challenge. God's confidence in Job is heard in Job 2:7-13. We learn of the disease which afflicts Job and of his wife's suggestion to curse God and die. In all this Job does not sin with his lips. Job knows nothing of God's action at the heavenly scene, but this way of presenting the case shows that God sometimes may allow suffering as a means of testing. God has confidence in the righteous man that he will endure and not sin in his afflictions.

Being an ancient story the Book of Job needed a happy ending. This is furnished in Job 42:7-17. Job's fortunes are restored and he lived to be an old man, full of days. Many wonder about this conclusion of the story, feeling that the climax in 42:1-6 is the proper ending. But there is a difficulty in leaving Job upon his ash heap as the storm subsides.

The Book of Job demands dramatic reading, for it is a dramatic masterpiece. The speeches need to be read in the spirit of those who are speaking. Each of the friends is distinct in his personality and his words should be read according to his mood. The reading of Job requires the flexibility which can express changing moods. The speeches of God mount up into majestic utterance. But it is in such reading that the book speaks its message most effectively.

4. ECCLESIASTES OR THE PREACHER

"Vanity of vanities! All is vanity!" This is the refrain of this book. This is the writer's report of his experience of life. "The end of the matter; all has been heard. Fear God, and keep his commandments; for this is the whole duty of man" (Eccles. 12:13). The author went through a whole series of experiments, testing the meaning of life. He went directly to life in a realistic manner. (1) Learning (Eccles. 1:12-18). He searched out wisdom, but found only that "in much wisdom is sorrow." (2) Pleasure (Eccles. 2:1-3). It proved nothing but vanity. (3) A great estate (Eccles. 2:4-11). But "behold, all was vanity and a striving after wind, and there was nothing to be gained under the sun."

The vanity of life produced despair and skepticism. In Ecclesiastes 3:12-26 this despair is fully expressed. One fate awaits the wise man and the fool: the wise man dies just like the fool. All the days of man are full of pain, and his work is a vexation. All is in the hands of God and God gives as he pleases. So the book continues in utter pessimism. There is only one positive statement, "Fear God, and keep his commandments." But this is said by one who has no hope in his fear of the Lord.

Why is this strange book in the Old Testament? Why does it stand in the midst of writings so full of rejoicing? There is the Book of Lamentations with its dirges in the days of the exile, but hope persisted. The writer of Ecclesiastes is not one cast down by afflictions caused by the oppressor. He is a man who is at sea in his thinking; knowledge becomes his curse, not his blessing. He had gone off the main road and was wandering up a dead-end path. He had lost personal contact with God in a maze of puzzling problems. But this book stands among The Writings. The skeptic is not excommunicated. His book is not burned. He remains among the saints, for he does have one real truth, "Fear God, and keep his commandments." The writer did not let his skepticism lead him into evil. He never arrived at the place of the fool who denied the presence and moral rule of God. (Ps. 14:1.) The mercy of God reaches even to this "gentle cynic."

5. THE SONG OF SONGS

This is a love lyric. Among the books of wisdom it seems strangely out of place. But perhaps it is well to place it here lest wisdom become too solemn. The Song of Songs is a beautiful, frankly expressed song of two ardent lovers. God is not mentioned. There is no attempt to impart wisdom. There is no moralizing either during the song or at its conclusion. It is full of the spirit of spring.

> "For lo, the winter is past,
>   the rain is over and gone.
> The flowers appear on the earth,
>   the time of singing has come" (S. of S. 2:11-12).

These two young lovers are confronted by the threat of the king to separate them, that he might have for himself this rose of Sharon, this lily of the valley. But "love is strong as death" and "many waters cannot quench love" (S. of S. 8:6-7). Many attempts have been made to interpret this book allegorically, but evidently the Old Testament was broad enough to include this beautiful lyric of true love which struggled against even the king.

6. SOLOMON AND THE WISDOM LITERATURE

The name of Solomon is always associated with the wisdom literature. Even a late, post-biblical book of the Greek period is called the Wisdom of Solomon. In 1 Kings 4:29-34 Solomon is eulogized for his wise sayings. Evidently he was a gatherer of proverbs and puzzles and was a coiner of the same. This places him at the head of the stream of proverbs. We have Moses and laws, David and psalms, Solomon and wisdom. Several of the collections within the Book of Proverbs have Solomon's name at the beginning. But Solomon's life did not manifest wisdom, however clever he may have been in coining wise sayings. His tyrannical folly produced a depression in Israel and resulted in the division of the kingdom. Wisdom did not come from King Solomon. This tyrant "in all his glory" was not arrayed like some of the humble, unnamed men whose wit and wisdom shine in their observations of life made in that fear of God which is the beginning and end of wisdom.

12

THAT THE SCRIPTURES MIGHT BE FULFILLED

"In many and various ways God spoke of old to our fathers by the prophets; but in these last days he has spoken to us by a Son" (Heb. 1:1).

THE CHRISTIAN TEACHER of the Old Testament stands within the revelation of God given in the New Testament. As he reads, studies, and teaches the Old Testament, he thinks in accordance with the truth of the New Testament. The Christian teacher uses the *whole* Bible, whose oneness, unity, and completeness are in the One God who makes himself known through its entirety. The same God is present and at work in both the Old Covenant and the New Covenant, in both the Old Testament and the New Testament.

The two testaments are bound together into the one Bible because the two covenants have been made by the same God. No personal preferences for the one or the other on the part of the reader are pertinent. Nor can the heresy be maintained that the God of the Old Testament is a God of love. In this regard, remember always that "his is a God of wrath, whereas the God of the New Testament love endures for ever." Each Testament sheds light on the other and each must be read for the sake of understanding the other.

The Old Testament gives the first steps in a work which is fulfilled in the New Testament. The whole is a mighty act of God for the salvation of all the people of the world. "Think not that I have come to abolish the law and the prophets; I have come not to abolish them but to fulfill them" (Matt. 5:17). This final chapter is still a study of the Old Testament; the questions it is concerned with are, "How can the New Testament help in understanding the Old Testament?" and "How can the Old Testament help in understanding the New Testament?"

1. THE OLD TESTAMENT AS A WHOLE IS FULFILLED IN THE NEW TESTAMENT

There is, as has been seen, a living wholeness, a dynamic oneness, in the Old Testament. Each item has meaning as being in some way a part of the whole. So, when some Old Testament verse is quoted, that verse must be seen in its relation to the whole. Each verse cited in reference to Jesus is a part of an entire section, of a whole book, of the whole Old Testament. It must not be detached from its setting to be used as a handy proof text: instead, it must be read and understood in relation to the whole revelation in the Old Testament. Jesus does not merely fulfill this verse or that verse, but as the Son of God he is the consummation of the whole.

For example, in Matthew's nativity story there occurs this comment regarding the flight into Egypt and return: "This was to fulfill what the Lord had spoken by the prophet, 'Out of Egypt have I called my son' " (Matt. 2:15). There is aptness in this citation, a confirmatory parallelism. But there is much more than that. The one who knows his Old Testament will go back to the prophet Hosea, that he may read these words as Hosea used them. That prophet of the Assyrian period, living in the days of the fast-approaching end of Ephraim, the Northern Kingdom, was employing his every God-given talent to persuade his people to return to God. He would have them return to God as a son returns to a father, because God had loved them as a father loves a son. Hosea's urgent plea contains one of the most moving declarations of the redemptive love of God:

> "Yet it was I who taught Ephraim to walk,
>   I took them up in my arms;
>   but they did not know that I healed them.
> I led them with cords of compassion,
>   with the bands of love,
> and I became to them as one
>   who eases the yoke on their jaws,
>   and I bent down to them and fed them" (Hos. 11:3-4).

That is the setting for the words of the prophet:

> "When Israel was a child, I loved him,
>   and out of Egypt I called my son" (Hos. 11:1).

After reading this one passage, one should turn back to the story of the calling of Israel out of Egypt. "And you shall say to Pharaoh, 'Thus says the Lord [Yahweh], Israel is my first-born son, and I say to you, "Let my son go that he may serve me"'" (Ex. 4:22). "My son" is a deep expression of redemptive love, of God's concern for his people. In the Exodus Story, God's love is directed toward his people in their bondage. In the prophet Hosea, God's love is directed toward his unfaithful, rebellious people. In Jesus, this love comes to its climax.

Therefore, when one reads Matthew's statement about the fulfillment of the Scripture words, "Out of Egypt have I called my son," he should see something far beyond a geographical reference. This citation of the utterance of a prophet yields its full biblical significance only when in reading it the believer recalls the mighty act of redemption when God called Israel out of Egypt to be his son and recalls also that message of urgent, appealing love which is the theme of Hosea. The One God reveals himself in the whole story of redemption, in the words of Moses, in the pleading of Hosea, and in the person of his Son. God's mercy, goodness, loving-kindness, steadfast love, and redeeming grace are the same yesterday, today, and forever. It is the Old Testament as a whole, not one passage only, which is fulfilled in this New Testament reference. The same is true of many other New Testament references.

The many statements in the New Testament about the Scriptures being fulfilled are not so many proof texts in support of Jesus' claim. The Son of God needs no proof texts to validate his Sonship. "I bear witness to myself, and the Father who sent me bears witness to me" (John 8:18). Instead of being proof texts, the citations from the Old Testament underscore at particular points what is true of the whole and so bind the two testaments together in the unifier, God himself. This can be seen in the Old Testament History, Law, and Prophets. It requires a review of the whole Old Testament under these three headings fully to appreciate this matter of fulfillment.

2. OLD TESTAMENT HISTORY IS FULFILLED IN THE NEW TESTAMENT

The Old Testament is a book of history. (See chap. 2 of this text.) It confronts the reader with accounts of God at work in specific acts in the earthly scene. Real history, real people, and real events in the affairs of families, tribes, and nations make up the stuff of this down-to-earth book. This history is recited in the Law, Prophets, and Psalms. It is a story which can be learned and narrated. It has a beginning and a continuity—the unfolding of vital processes in the life of people. It can be laid out on a time line. But the story does not come to completion in the Old Testament.

If we had only the history as given in the Old Testament, the story would seem to come to a dead end, as will be seen by reading the end of the Book of Nehemiah. However, one of the most striking features of the Old Testament is its spirit of great expectations. For Israel there always was some hitherto unrealized act of God just ahead. Hope was always present. This hope, when contradicted, persistently revived. The chosen people were ever forward-looking. This feeling did not arise from Israel's confidence in national power, but from Israel's trust in God. "Hope in God!" was the awakening cry in every affliction (Ps. 42:5). But this hope did not come to its realization in the Old Testament. The Old Testament, however, is not the end of the story.

The New Testament also is a book of history. It also confronts the reader with the account of God at work in specific acts on the earthly scene. "The Word became flesh and dwelt among us" (John 1:14). The history which was begun in the Old Testament and which was carried on over such a long stretch of time was consummated in a historical person, Jesus, and in a historical event, the Cross. In this person and this event, the Old Testament reaches a completion which unfolds its meaning.

Both of these recitals of history are necessary. The New Testament history is deeply understood only when the whole Old Testament story enters deeply into the mind of the believer. What God did in his Son, Jesus the Christ, is rightly apprehended only when as believers we know God as he revealed himself in the entirety of his dealings with Israel. We must recall God's work of creation in the beginning and his choosing of Abraham and his family that he might bless them and make them a blessing; we must celebrate anew God's miracle of salvation at the Red Sea, when God called his chosen people out of bondage and made his covenant with them in steadfast love. We must follow God as he works through all the tragedies and deliverances and join in the new song of redemption when the exiles are brought out of captivity. We must see God at work in the underground, as the saints are made to pass through the fiery furnace. Learning this history is much more than an exercise in memorization; it is seeing with "the eyes of faith" and so participating in the experience of Israel in its wholeness. Such recital, when woven deeply into the consciousness, gives the right state of mind for reading the New Testament.

On the other hand, the Old Testament history is best understood when the mind of the reader is informed and oriented by the New Testament story. But the reader of the New Testament must not carry back into the minds of Old Testament characters that fullness of knowledge which came with Jesus, neither may he judge those characters and their conduct by the new standard given by Jesus. In the processes of history, each man belongs to a certain generation and period. Each is limited according to his stage of partial, incomplete comprehension. The test questions are: "Is this man headed in the right direction? Is he facing toward the day?" That can be determined only by complete revelation in the Son. The Old Testament as a whole presents the pilgrimage of Israel under the guiding word of God both in judgment and in promise. This is the whole that is fulfilled in the Son. In the Cross all the tragedies and deliverances of Israel are seen in the light of God's purposes, which is one of redeeming love. In the history of the Son of God we find the fulfillment of God's intention in the whole of the Old Testament history.

3. THE OLD TESTAMENT LAW IS FULFILLED IN THE NEW TESTAMENT

The Old Testament is a book of Law. Moses, the Law-giver, stands pre-eminent in the Old Covenant. The reading of the Old Testament is not complete without close attention to the laws contained therein. There are three great codes. (See Ex. 20:1—27:19; Lev. 17:1—26:46; Deut. 13:1—26:19.) There are other rules besides these, but in these three large blocks of civil-religious regulations are found the basic laws of Israel. The Hebrew word *Torah,* which is translated Law, means instruction. The Law of God in these codes is God's direction for living together as God's people. By statutes and ordinances God was at work instructing and disciplining Israel in its daily life.

These codes should be read to see the everyday life of Israel in their towns and villages, with all the various contacts of neighbor with neighbor, and the tensions and questions of right and wrong. A group living together has constant problems of interrelationship. With imagination the reader can see back of these laws the people themselves. These laws are not regulations imposed upon a people from without, but are the ways by which they discovered God's will for their life as a people of God. At the heart of these codes there is a strong conviction of justice, a sense of equalitarian rights among a people who stand before their God with no class distinctions. There is a simple democracy based on the worth of each individual. Through all, there is a constant awareness of God's loving-kindness and fidelity to his covenant, which binds the people into covenant relations with him and also with one another.

Another important factor is the strong motivation of the love of God which saves this legislation from becoming mere legalism. Note the beginning of the Exodus code, with its reminder of how God delivered his people from bondage in Egypt: "I am the Lord your God, who brought you out of the land of Egypt, out of the house of bondage" (Ex. 20:2). Such is the motivation for the observance of these laws. The Leviticus code contains this often repeated phrase: "You will be holy; for I the Lord your God am holy" (Lev. 19:1, etc.); or "I am the Lord your God" (Lev. 18:1, etc.); or simply, "I am the Lord" (Lev. 18:5, etc.). In Deuteronomy, the code of laws is in a setting of eloquent exhortations which aim to create the true fear of God, i. e., awe and gratitude. These codes of law are rightly understood only when seen in their practical directions for living together as a simple, agricultural people. Reading these seldom-read codes with appreciative, re-creative imagination is an enlightening experience.

By all these directions, motivated by true devotion to God, accepted in genuine piety, Israel was formed into a unique community, a distinct people, with a God-given function in the world. Under Ezra and the scribes, the study and observance of the Law was organized in a thorough program of educaton filled with the songs of praises of The Psalms. Psalm 1 shows the blessedness of the observer of the Law. The instructed Jew sang with deep joy,

> "Oh, how I love thy law!
> It is my meditation all the day" (Ps. 119:97).

This elaborate "Psalm of the Law" should accompany the reading of the codes. In each of the twenty-two alphabetical sections, one or more of many synonymous words are used: law, testimonies, ways, precepts, statutes, commandments, ordinances. The Law was all of these. The pious Jew loved the Law, meditated upon it, prized it as God's peculiar gift to Israel.

Besides these practical directions for daily life, there were the laws pertaining to worship. These regulations had to do with the sabbath, sacrifices, and all sorts of ritualistic matters. Under the demands of the priesthood, the laws of sacrifice were elaborated and made into a heavy burden. Under the legalism of the scribes, there developed a multiplicity of rules and interpretations which became a yoke too heavy to be borne. This legalism interfered with direct personal relations with God. Keeping the rules was said to be the way of gaining the favor of God. The works of the Law were declared to be the way of salvation. Thus, a system of legalism was developed which was an obstacle to that true piety which rests on the grace of God. The reader of the Old Testament must go back of this legalism of the Pharisees to the old codes, if he is to understand the Law as God's instructions for his people.

Jesus grew up in the Law and spoke to a people who lived in this Law. He saw the true piety of those who loved the Law. Of Nathaniel he said, "Behold, an Israelite indeed, in whom is no guile" (John 1:47). Jesus saw in the Ten Commandments the abiding Law of God. But he recognized that the whole Law could be summarized in two of its commandments. This is an illuminating instance of fulfillment.

> "And one of them, a lawyer, asked him a question, to test him, 'Teacher, which is the great commandment in the law?' and he said to him, 'You shall love the Lord your God with all your heart, and with all your soul, and with all your mind. This is the great and first commandment. And the second is like it, You shall love your neighbor as yourself. On these two commandments depend all the law and the prophets'" (Matt. 22:34-40).

These two commandments are important in the study of the Old Testament, for both are quoted from the Old Testament Law. The first is from the *Shema* (Deut. 6:5) and the second is found in the Holiness Code (Lev. 19:18). Jesus, as a reader of the whole Old Testament, had the discrimination to recognize among all its laws these two which contain all in essence. The old Law contained within itself that which Jesus recognized as its fulfillment. As Jesus quotes these two essential Laws, which summarize the Law, the reader of the Old Testament is given a clue to the meaning of the Law. Now he can see in all its multiplicity of details what God was doing through these codes. He can see that God was at work awakening the love of his people toward himself and toward one another. This was the twofold purpose of God in giving the Law. With that clue in mind, the three codes should be reread.

Laws tend toward legalism. A set of commandments written upon stone tablets may become a mere set of external requirements to be obeyed in order to gain right relations with God. A slave morality results, in which there is no heart, no mind, no love. Motivation is all important. That is evident in the *Shema* and in all three of the codes. In them obedience is based upon God's redemptive love. Here Jesus brought the Law to its fulfillment. "A new commandment I give you, that you love one another; even as I have loved you, that you also love one another" (John 13:34). The Son of God himself, in laying down his life as the good shepherd lays down his life for the sheep, becomes a motivating force. The old Law, stated in the two commandments, is made new by the new dynamic of Christ's love. What was inherent in all the Law because God gave it, is made so vital and creative in the Son that it becomes a *new* commandment.

Jesus interpreted the Law. Seven ways in which he fulfilled the Law by his new interpretation are as follows: (1) By preserving them. "Not an iota, not a dot, will pass from the law until all is accomplished" (Matt. 5:18). There is enduring value in the whole and in every part. (2) By superseding such temporary regulations as those regarding clean and unclean animals and the ritual of the Temple. (3) By freeing the laws from the accumulated additions of the traditions of men (Mark 7:1-23). (4) By transforming what needed remaking, such as the laws regarding swearing and those regarding just retribution (Matt. 5:33-42). (5) By deepening the meaning of the truth in the old, as in the commandments regarding murder (Matt. 5:21-26; 33:39). (6) By unifying the multiplicity of the whole into the one commandment of love (Matt. 22:35-40; John 13:34-35). (7) By making men free as children of God (Gal. 5:1).

4. The Old Testament Prophets Are Fulfilled in the New Testament

As the long list of prophets is reviewed, from Moses down to the close of the prophetic period, the first impression we have of these men is of their independence. They were independent of kings, priests, and one another. No prophet quotes another or looks to anyone else for authority or support. They were, one and all, marked by rugged individualism. There was no official or academic succession. In the priesthood, a man held his position because of his ancestry. He was born a priest. Among the scribes, there was the succession of teacher and pupil. The rabbis, with deferential humility, quoted the rabbis before them. A prophet, however, was directly called of God. He spoke out of his own meeting with God. Amos declared: "I am no prophet, nor a prophet's son . . . the Lord took me . . . the Lord said to me, 'Go prophesy to my people Israel'" (Amos 7:14-15). Each Hebrew *nabi* (prophet) spoke as though a spontaneous eruption was breaking out within him.

"There is in my heart as it were a burning fire
   shut up in my bones,
and I am weary with holding it in,
   and I cannot" (Jer. 20:9).

Each prophet spoke out of his intense personal experience. And each spoke in accordance with his own peculiar individuality. They had no body of doctrine. They were not educated in any systematic theology. To his own generation, the prophet seemed to be a heretic guilty of subversive teaching. They were independents, nonconformists, protestants, disturbers of the peace of the rulers. The differences of these markedly individual nonconformists make them a succession without any outward uniformity.

But there was an inward unity which made them the real company of the prophets. They were messengers called by God himself, appointed to speak his word with authority. "Thus says the Lord" was their authentic word. "Full of the spirit of the Lord" was another distinguishing mark. When they are viewed in their historical order, seen performing their succession of assignments, the whole prophetic movement can be comprehended. These emphatic proclaimers of God in period after period of Israel's history seem like the successive footprints of God as he marches down the centuries. Viewed in perspective, they reveal the path of God which was like a shining light, the light of dawn, that shines more and more, brighter and brighter, until the full day, the perfect day. (See Proverbs 4:18 in both the K.J.V. and the R.S.V.). It is this prophetic whole, so rich in its individual differences, which is fulfilled in the New Testament.

"In many and various ways [At sundry times and in divers manners—K.J.V.] God spoke of old to our fathers by the prophets; but in these last days he has spoken to us by a Son" (Heb. 1:1). So the prophets and the Son are differentiated and also bound together. The prophets are the spokesmen of God filled with his spirit: The Son is the spokesman of God filled with his Spirit. So the Son is the climax, the completer, the interpreter of the prophets. In the Son, the believer rereads the prophets, perceiving the unifying and unfolding truth which was in each one and in the movement as a whole. On his walk to Emmaus, Jesus said to his unrecognizing friends: "O foolish men, and slow of heart to believe all that the prophets have spoken! Was it not necessary that the Christ should suffer these things and enter into his glory? And beginning with Moses and all the prophets, he interpreted to them in all the scriptures the things concerning himself" (Luke 24:25-27). How much we wish that we had that discourse, to learn how Jesus interpreted the prophets as a whole!

In four passages we can see the Son's fulfilling of the prophets as a whole. Luke quotes the passage from Isaiah which Jesus used in the Nazareth synagogue.

"The Spirit of the Lord is upon me,
    because he has anointed me to preach good news to the poor.
He has sent me to proclaim release to the captives
    and recovering of sight to the blind,
    to set at liberty those who are oppressed,
    to proclaim the acceptable year of the Lord" (Luke 4:18-19).

After the reading, Jesus added, "Today this scripture has been fulfilled in your hearing." Jesus quoted Isaiah 61:1-2. The Son is the Spirit-filled prophet. He proclaims glad tidings of emancipation, he proclaims the year of the Lord. At the core of every prophetic message is this proclamation of the day of righteousness, the day of God's setting affairs right among men. God's righteousness and justice are central in the preaching of the prophets. Jesus fulfills them when he establishes righteousness and justice.

Recall Jesus' two summary commandments: "You shall love the Lord your God with all your heart, and with all your soul, and with all your mind" and "You shall love your neighbor as yourself" (Matt. 22:37, 39). The question put to Jesus was regarding the Law, "Teacher, which is the great commandment in the law?" But after giving his answer, Jesus declares, "On these two commandments depend [hang] all the law *and the prophets.*" This twofold statement of God's will, therefore, is not only the summary of the law as a whole, but also of the prophets as a whole. Jesus affirms that the whole work of the prophets was to lead his people to love God and to love one another. In the light of these words of the fulfiller of the Scriptures, the words of the prophets are illuminated. The will of God was back of and pervaded all their utterances. Micah expressed this mind of God in his statement of what God requires: "To do justice and to love kindness, and to walk humbly with your God" (Micah 6:8). This, in brief, is the whole of the prophets. The Son fulfills this.

Another very significant word of Jesus is his twice-quoted word from Hosea, "I desire mercy and not sacrifice" (Matt. 9:13 and 12:7). Turning back to that prophet, we find this word in the midst of a protest against the thoughtless way in which Ephraim was returning to the Lord. To them it seemed to be just a matter of making a sacrifice upon an altar. But Hosea protests, "For I desire steadfast love [recall that key word *hesed*] and not sacrifice, the knowledge of God, rather than burnt offerings." This, as we saw in the chapters on the prophets, is at the core of the teachings of all the great prophets. (See Amos 5:21-25; Isa. 1:11-17; Micah 6:6-8; Jer. 7:21-23; Ps. 51:16-17.) This is the living word of God, active, sharper than any two-edged sword, piercing, discerning the thoughts and intentions of the heart.

Consider Jesus' heart-searching words in the Sermon on the Mount (Matt. 5:21-26). The Master is speaking about bad relations, of hatred for one another, of murder, anger, sarcasm, and quarrels. "If you are offering your gift at the altar, and there remember that your brother has something against you, leave your gift there before the altar and go; first be reconciled to your brother, and then come and offer your gift. Make friends quickly with your accuser." "I desire mercy, not sacrifice." This law, both old and new, was spoken when men felt that religion was essentially the offering of sacrifices on the altar. The prophets penetrated into the real nature of religion as loving God and loving one another, walking humbly before God, and doing justice. Here also Jesus fulfills the prophets.

But the greatest of all the words of the prophets fulfilled by the Son are those in Isaiah, chap. 53. This is the profoundest passage in Hebrew prophecy. It is a very surprising passage. The chapters immediately preceding this one, sound forth an awakening call to Israel, the servant of the Lord, assuring her that her deliverance is at hand. In Isaiah 52:1-11, Zion is called to awaken and to depart from Babylon. Then there is a surprising turn in the prophetic message, an amazing swing upward, beyond anything which has gone before, as the prophet confronts Israel with the one upon whom the Lord laid the iniquity of us all. The whole section is Isaiah 52:13—53:12. The chapter arrangement is poor here. The reading should begin at 52:13: "Behold my servant shall prosper, he shall be exalted. . . ." The proper heading would be, "The Exaltation of the Suffering Servant." Vicarious love is the true glory.

This passage, so surprising in its setting, rising so far above and beyond men's thinking, was a dark saying to Israel. They did not comprehend it. Their perplexity is seen in the case of the Ethiopian student of the Word. "Do you understand what you are reading?" inquired Philip. "How can I, unless some one guides me?" "About whom,

pray, does the prophet say this, about himself or about
some one else?" (See Acts 8:26-39.) The perplexity of the
Ethiopian was natural. The rabbis of that day had no satis-
factory interpretation to give to this pupil. They were
without an explanation and were asking the same questions. But Philip had the clue. He had seen one actually
led to the slaughter for the transgression of the world, just
as this chapter had described him. And then this suffering
servant had been highly exalted. Jesus, giving his life
for the sins of the world and rising again in glory, made
this chapter clear to Philip. It became luminous with its
full meaning. It was no longer a dark saying. This profoundest passage had not been a help in anticipating the
Savior of the world. But the Cross made it clear. Now it
was fulfilled. After Jesus' death on the Cross, the followers
of Jesus turned back to this amazing passage with understanding. As the Christian reads Isaiah 52:13—53:12, he
finds that it sheds light on Jesus because Jesus sheds light
on it. Jesus fulfilled it by actually being vicarious love
and by actually being exalted. See the rewriting of this
truth in Philippians 2:5-11. Paul had his mind full of
Isaiah's portrayal of the true servant of the Lord and also
full of the story of the Cross and the Resurrection. They
are like two sides of the same impression of the truth.

Messiah is an important term. *Messiah* is the Hebrew
word. *Christ* is the Greek word. *Anointed* is the Latin
word. All mean the same. It was an ancient custom to
pour oil on the head of an official, priest, or king to denote
his consecration (1 Sam. 10:1, 16:13). A man so anointed
was called *Messiah* in Hebrew, *Christos* in Greek. In Isaiah
45:1, Cyrus is called the anointed of the Lord, that is,
Messiah, Christos. As the prophets looked for the rule of
God to be established, they hoped for an ideal ruler, one
who was truly the anointed. As Israel suffered more and

more under the great world powers, this hope grew stronger. But all sorts of ideas got into men's minds. The best is found in Isaiah 9:6-7 and 11:1-5. But in Jesus' day, the longing for a national military ruler was predominant. So Jesus had trouble with this term. He had to fill it with meaning by his own words, works, and life. He had to remake the thinking of his people regarding the Christ, the Messiah. He fulfills this expectation by radically remaking it.

The Christian reader of the Old Testament stands in the truth of the New Testament. He believes in the One God who speaks in both Testaments. Hence, his aim as a student is to know both, so that each may illuminate the other. Both are Holy Scriptures.